D0318933

Supportive Schools

Case studies for teachers and other professionals working in schools

Tony Charlton and Kenneth David

MACMILLAN
EDUCATION

Edge Hill College
Learning Resource Centre

Author CHARLTON

Class No. 371.9

Book No. 339272

©Tony Charlton and Kenneth David 1990

All rights reserved. No reproduction, copy or transmission
of this publication may be made without written permission.

No paragraph of this publication may be reproduced, copied
or transmitted save with written permission or in accordance
with the provisions of the Copyright, Designs and Patents Act 1988.
The photocopying of some pages is permitted. These pages are
marked P . However, only reasonable quantities of
photocopies can be made and these should be for internal school
use only, or for use in small-scale in-service or pre-service courses
conducted by LEAS and colleges. Under no circumstances can
large numbers of copies by made by schools, LEAS or colleges.

Any person who does any unauthorised act in relation to
this publication may be liable to criminal prosecution and
civil claims for damages.

Published by
MACMILLAN EDUCATION LTD
Houndmills, Basingstoke, Hampshire RG21 2XS
and London
Companies and representatives
throughout the world

Printed in Hong Kong

British Library Cataloguing in Publication Data
Supportive schools: case studies for teachers and other
  professionals working in schools.
  1. Great Britain. Schools. Students with special
  education needs. Counselling
  I. Charlton, Tony   II. David, Kenneth
  371.9

ISBN 0-333-49619-1

CONTENTS

young child's deafness can be helped through a Health Visitor's work.

4   Jeremy   20

A change in a Primary School child's disruptive behaviour. An examination of the possible reasons for the dramatic improvements in a
young boy's behaviour after his prior disruptive behaviour had caused
real concern both at home and in school.

5   James   28

An eight-year-old boy with specific learning difficulties – dyslexia.

6 Patrick

Possible child abuse. A teacher is concerned about an older Primary age child's physical injuries and the possibility that he is being abused at home. The teacher encounters the dilemma of making a decision about whether or not to share her concern with others.

7 Sally

An epileptic person fit for work. This deals with the Primary and Secondary School career of a young girl with epilepsy, and her later adult work.

8 Sandra

A thirteen-year-old child in a special school has severe learning difficulties.

13 Tommy   95

A route for a misfit. This case study illustrates how a Secondary School's pastoral care provision and practices can fail to help some youngsters.

14 Savas   106

Low self-esteem in a Secondary School child. This study deals with the case of a child with a history of poor achievement and low self-esteem.

15 Clearview High School   118

In-Service Training in personal and social education. The staff of a secondary school can be helped through In-Service Training to be better tutors and to work in a more integrated pastoral system.

INTRODUCTION

This book presents fifteen varied case studies which range over the professional practices of teachers, and professionals from other agencies concerned with schoolchildren. It illustrates attempts to meet the personal needs of young people in pre-school provision, in Primary and Secondary schools, and in Special schools. It is intended to help professional staff whose responsibilities are directed towards helping children and young adults.

The material emphasises good intervention practices and the theory which underpins such actions. While the main focus of all these case studies is in the school, many involve a wide range of personnel from other agencies – the school psychological service, health visitors, education welfare officers, psychiatrists, social workers, probation officers, support teachers, speech therapists, counsellors, physiotherapists and voluntary agencies.

The editors argue that students' and practitioners' professional competence can be enhanced not only by being given theoretical guidelines about a range of appropriate pastoral intervention strategies, but also by studying practical examples of their use, particularly where a multi-professional approach is required. Theory and practice must work in tandem. Our experiences have strongly suggested that practising and trainee teachers can benefit from the use of 'templates' which can illustrate both theory and practice and provide flexible blueprints for possible future action.

The case studies have come partly from our own experience and partly from colleagues in teaching and other professions. We have necessarily altered some details to preserve privacy, but all the work is based on real situations.

Suggested methods for using the material

Each case study has a **QUESTIONS** section which may help individual readers or leaders of student and professional discussion groups.

All the studies also have a **SUPPORTIVE INFORMATION AND MATERIAL** section.

(a) Much of this material outlines the roles of the professional workers involved and the assessment, intervention and evaluation procedures and practices which are used to identify and meet an individual pupil's needs.

(b)   Other supplementary material may be less factual and require thought and discussion on possible lines of action.

(c)   Most case studies indicate useful reference material and further reading.

(d)   Some of the supplementary material offers certain parallel ideas and material which is only loosely associated with the theme of the case study. These items are intended to provide further ideas for study, discussion and training sessions, and may add wider-ranging considerations.

(e)   Material which may be photocopied without reference to the editors or publishers, providing acknowledgement is made on the reproductions, is indicated as follows ⊡ .

Teachers in all types of schools should find much material for use in their school In-Service Training days, and lecturers and students in differing pre-professional studies will have material for a variety of work concerned with special educational needs, and with other more general educational issues.

We hope that individual readers will also find the studies useful for their personal study and reflection.

ACKNOWLEDGEMENTS

Substantial contributions from the following are gratefully acknowledged:
Jo Barrett – Case study 3
Barbara Brown – Case study 2
Julie Franklin – Case study 12
Lynne Hoye – Case study 14
Joyce James – Case study 11
Joyce Johnson – Case study 5
Ian Leech – Case study 10
Tony Oliver – Case study 7
John Presland – Case study 8
Ian Pike – Case study 14 Supplementary Material
Kate Wall – Case study 1
Charles Wise – Book list in Case study 13

The author and publishers wish to thank the following for permission to use copyright material: Lifeskills Associates Ltd for table, 'Lifeskills: Taking Charge of yourselves and your life', Lifeskills Teaching Programme.

Every effort has been made to trace all the copyright holders but if any have been inadvertently overlooked the publishers will be pleased to make the necessary arrangement at the first opportunity.

The Turners

Attempts to meet the individual needs of a young child entering Infant School

The role of the Home–School Link (or Liaison) teachers referred to in this study is complex, for each responds, often in differing ways, to the individual needs of their own area. These teachers are directly responsible to the Headteacher of the local school to which they are attached. Their role is to promote, and encourage, improved links between the home, the school and other professional agencies.

This case study begins with a Home–School Link teacher from a school in an area of high unemployment – with many single-parent families living in council property (a mixture of houses and flats) – visiting a family. From information provided by the local Child Health Department the teacher knew the family included a child, David, who would be of school age the following September. The family of Mum, Dad and four children, were living in a two-bedroomed flat on the third floor of a large three-storey block of flats. Dad was unemployed, the family finances were in poor shape, and they could not afford to pay for playgroup fees for either David or Claire, his sister, who is 12 months his junior. During the teacher's initial visit the parents were both communicative and friendly and shared their concern about Claire's poor speech. Claire was not a shy child and talked readily to the visitor, demonstrating very unclear and nasal speech and poor language development.

The parents had already spoken to the Health Visitor and she was monitoring Claire's progress. The teacher offered to speak to the Health Visitor and find out what help was appropriate and available. The parents seemed relieved and welcomed her additional support. They told her of their fight to be housed in a three-bedroomed house with a garden, and asked if she would also support them on that count. From an educational standpoint it was obvious that the housing problem, together with a lack of playgroup experience and a speech problem would hinder Claire's future school progress. The teacher felt that if her help, on both counts, would assist in any way, then she would be providing help for Claire's specific needs and improving her chances of later success in school.

On initial contact the Health Visitor was not openly receptive and questioned the teacher's role and reasons for 'interfering'. When the teacher explained that, in her professional capacity, she was interested in the needs of the child then relations improved. Over a short period of time the relationship between the two agency workers continued to improve and, once mutual respect had been established, their involvement complemented each other. The Health Visitor expressed her own concerns about Claire's apparent speech delay and was willing to support both a referral to a local Medical Officer and an appeal to the local Housing Department.

After a period of two months during which many telephone calls were made and many letters written the outcome was that the family were offered, and accepted, a house. Letters had been sent to both the Housing Department and supportive members of the Housing Committee.

Claire was assessed by the Medical Officer a month later. A Griffiths Developmental Assessment was completed and Claire's poor hand/eye co-ordination and language/speech delay were particularly noted. Using this assessment to claim much-needed support for Claire the Home–School Link teacher was able to obtain funding from the Social Services Department for Claire to attend a playgroup. Social Services agreed that the inadequacies within the family were limiting Claire's development, and that guided play would both encourage and develop Claire's personal, intellectual and social skills.

Through medical follow-up Claire underwent tonsillectomy, adenoidectomy and insertion of one grommet later that year.

The combination of the medical treatment and playgroup attendance has helped to resolve many of Claire's problems and it is now felt she will be able to settle, and progress well, when she attends primary school. By working across the boundaries between the relevant professional agencies, multi-agency expertise has combined to give Claire the help needed to start school on an equal footing with her peers.

QUESTIONS

1   What provision is there for children who do not have a school educational 'outreach' facility such as a Home–School Link teacher?

2   Do professionals, as part of their training, learn of the roles of the related agencies and is this best included in basic training or in In-Service training?

3   How much opportunity do we have to meet other professional agency personnel? How can this best be arranged, bearing in mind busy time-tables?

4   What links are useful or necessary with local authority Housing Officers?

5   How far should families be helped, and how far motivated to act for themselves? Can too caring an involvement by support services produce dependency?

6   As teachers in general (but specifically Pastoral and Home–School Link teachers) are faced with responding to an immense variety of school-related problems, should they all have a fundamental knowledge of counselling skills/techniques? Should it be included in basic training?

SUPPORTIVE INFORMATION AND MATERIAL

1   Agencies involved

Home–School Link teacher – Local Education Department, County Council.
Health Visitor – Local Health Authority.
Child Health Department – Local Health Authority.
Medical Officer – Local Health Authority.
Local Hospital – Local Health Authority.
Housing Department – Local Council.
Social Services Department – County Council.
Local Councillors – Local Council.

Pre-School Playgroups Association
  Head Office, 61–3 Kings Cross Road,
  London WC1X 9LL.
  Telephone 071 833 0991
  (For information about local branches.)

2 Common children's health problems met by teachers

Acne and skin trouble – eczema Dyslexia
Overweight and diet needs Puberty – first stage of adolescence
Clumsiness Sexual Maturation
Tiredness Growth spurts at different ages
Eyesight difficulties Menstruation
Hearing difficulties Fears of isolation
Asthma Developing temperament and personality
Epilepsy Anxiety and sensitivity over body image.

3 What are the essential needs of children?

Security.
Acceptance by, and of, others
Sensitivity and control of one's feelings and of others' feelings.
Ability to look, listen, read, write and talk competently.
Health, proper sleep, enjoyable activity and friendship of others.
Some aesthetic appreciation of music and art.
Some lifelong curiosity about people and things.
Affection from, and for, others.
Self-awareness of one's abilities.
Comprehending society and one's place in it.
Standards which give values to live by, and a philosophy for one's existence.
Gradual responsibility and co-operation with others.
A lively and stimulating education, some adequate qualifications, and reasonable success in ambitions.

4 Could the following be a personal list of our adult needs?

What could each item mean in detail? How many link back to childhoood?

- Health
- Security and privacy
- Giving and receiving affection
- Feeling worthwhile

- Ambition and drive
- Learning and qualifications
- Skills
- Values and maturity

5 Might maturity be:

- the capacity to accept and depend on self
- to cease from identifying with others
- to rely on one's own standards
- to aspire towards a personal ideal
- to be capable of detaching oneself from social demands – to stand 'outside' our customary setting?

6 Are these commonly agreed values?

- Appropriate care of the young
- Knowledge of the need to share and co-operate with others throughout life.
- Understanding of the need for love and respect in relationships.
- Acceptance of the need to value and control sexual feelings.
- Care in preventing or reducing unhappiness?
- The maximising of happiness, for pleasure can be a value.
- To seek fulfilment in knowledge, as an intrinsic value, the better to know what should be chosen or avoided.

7 Useful reading

DAVID, K and CHARLTON T. (1987) *The Caring Role of the Primary School* (Basingstoke: Macmillan Education).

DAVID, K. and WILLIAMS, T. (eds) (1987) *Health Education in Schools* (London: Harper and Row).

KIRBY, N. (1981) *Personal Values in Primary Education* (London: Harper and Row).

WHITFIELD R. (1985) *Families Matter* (Basingstoke: Marshall Pickering).

Matthew

*A disorganised child in a
Primary School*

Matthew is six years old with a balanced height–weight ratio for a boy of his age and no apparent physical disability. He is not an articulate child and on closer examination his receptive, interpretive and expressive language is a weak link in his learning. He frequently draws attention to himself when he fails to understand a task through noisy, disruptive behaviour, by exhibiting an over-confidence or displaying obvious signs of boredom and disinterest.

Dressing

Matthew brings a sense of disorder to the movement learning environment by his appearance, with his shoes on the wrong feet, and being untidily dressed and frequently in a state of part undress because his attempts to button, lace, find sleeves, identify the top, front/back of garments have failed, often causing frustration to the child and his teacher. When he has undressed for Physical Education his untidy heap of clothes conveys much about his problem. Sleeves, trouser legs, socks are inside out or lost inside the garment, shoes are unfastened and the clothes are in a tangle, and so when dressing commences following the lesson the scene is one of frustration, disorder and chaos. Although he is at first left to cope with the dressing problems he has created, eventually an adult helps to dress him.

Movement of self

Matthew conveys disorder in his movements and in the way he moves. He gives an appearance of being rushed and this scrambled effect spills over to create a movement 'mess'. He usually generates more chaos by tripping, falling and bumping into other children or objects. An inability to co-ordinate move ments and exert the required degree of effort results in a lack of control in both fine and gross movement tasks.

Movement with others

His attempts to interact with other children in a movement context, with and without apparatus, are fraught with difficulties and result in disharmony and discord in an infant class Physical Education lesson. In an open and unstable environment further difficulties of a temporal and spatial nature become apparent.

Movement understanding

Matthew demonstrates a lack of understanding in terms of the movement task and in his performances. First, he should be helped to understand the essential requirements of the task, as well as helped to perceive the task as a whole in order to conceive the purpose and how to perform it. The teacher needs to illustrate the task as a whole in a meaningful context, and then analyse it into sequential steps to provide an order. The 'steps' can be developed through the use of action words and/or body parts, and these should be limited to 1–4 words. This enables Matthew to establish a beginning, middle and end to the task, and while he is performing he can match the words with the actions. The teacher can make the steps to achievement as small or large as is appropriate, and he/she can progressively adapt them in order that success is assured. This approach helps Matthew to feel secure in the learning environment and with time he will look upon the teacher as an 'enabler', who provides stepping-stones for him to follow during the learning of a task. At first Matthew may only achieve the first step but with adaptation and guidance gradually more steps will be negotiated, and he will enjoy a sense of achievement during the incremental stages. This approach allows the teacher to simplify and reduce the learning demands for Matthew so that he can begin to learn with success. It also helps to focus his attention on each necessary step in order to secure achievement. The sequential steps are visually encoded through a process of look, listen, say and do and supplemented with tactile guidance which helps to activate the short-term memory, so that Matthew will eventually be able (visually, verbally and through movement) to recall the sequence of the task. The teacher then has to work towards Matthew recalling and utilising the task appropriately in a more 'open' learning environment.

Another dimension of movement understanding is for Matthew to know how he is performing in the context of the task. Frequently, a child with movement learning difficulties has little or no idea of how he/she is performing in terms of it being appropriate and successful, or how to modify his performance in order to achieve success. The child's behaviour conveys a lack of knowing and 'feel' for the movement. The kinaesthetic sense is usually underdeveloped and in some cases undeveloped. This sense is an integral part of the proprioceptive sense and is concerned with the development of the right degree of effort, tension, stretch and orientation of the body and limbs required in the execution of a movement task. The teacher is presented with the responsibility for developing this sense and it can to some degree be achieved through the utilisation of the senses. For example, *vision*, where the child watches and then copies the teacher, so that gradually the mismatch between the two performances is resolved. Through *audition*, where the child listens and then matches the meaning that the word and its sound conveys with the action. Finally, through *touch*, where the teacher can guide the child through the movement pattern and where he can learn to feel the effort, tension, stretch and orientation of the body and limb(s) conveyed via the teacher. A child with movement learning difficulties is often in a state of hypo or hyper tension when he is in a movement context that requires precision and control. The teacher's capacity to help him establish the right degree of tension is crucial, and if the demands of the learning environment are appropriate so that the child knows he is secure and able to achieve, then this will go a long way towards allowing him to function with increasingly more ease and fluency. To create, at will, a sense of stretch, an increase or decrease of tension is something that this type of child cannot easily do, and yet he is required to in many movement situations in school. It gradually has to be learned with the help of the teacher through the development of the kinaesthetic sense. This sense is central to the development of movement control in fine and gross movement tasks and when interacting, co-operating and moving sensitively with a partner, within a small group or class.

Personal and social education considerations

During his third year at school Matthew is already exhibiting behaviours associated with failure! Hidden under a cloak of boisterous over-confidence and sometimes angry/frustrated behaviour is a lack of confidence and self-worth in a movement context. Movement permeates life and so he is going to be exposed increasingly to failure as the movement situations become more demanding. Matthew's disorganised, uncoordinated and uncontrolled movement behaviour is affecting his relationship with children in his class, his teacher and parents in play, school work and home situations. He is experiencing a sense of inadequacy, distress and alienation due to his movement learning difficulty, that requires immediate help from his teacher and parents, with guidance and support from the LEA Advisory and Support Services. Negative and inappropriate behaviour in the form of opting out, withdrawing into himself, seeking diversions, distractibility, inattention, disruption, tension and frustration are behaviours associated with Matthew and all these will slowly dissipate as soon as an appropriate teaching strategy, programme and environment is constructed and implemented in the school and home. For children like Matthew movement can create unhappy experiences, yet normally for the young child it is associated with pleasure, fun and enjoyment. Matthew inevitably brings the fear of failure to learning and play, and this only exacerbates the failure cycle because the sense of fear impairs his capacity to learn and perform. Instead of functioning at a near optimum level of arousal he tends to be in either a hypo or hyper aroused state which impairs cognition (the sensory, perceptual-cognitive, neuro-motor process).

Possible causes

Matthew's movement learning difficulties could be:

> a result of problems in the pre, para or post natal stage of development, impoverishment within the home and social environment or concomitant learning difficulties.
>
> (Brown and Baker, 1989, p. 1)

Movement observation, assessment and recording

The assessment process should include a comprehensive and in-depth analysis of the child in a variety of situations. It should also include an analysis of the appropriateness of the teaching strategy, learning environment, task and objectives and curriculum. The teacher/parents should also be prepared to assess their role, practice and responsibility for the learning environment in order to increase their effectiveness as enablers of learning. Assessment should be a continuous aspect of the teaching–learning process that allows for the gathering and reviewing of movement learning information on the child by a variety of methods, and in as wide a range of situations as possible (namely home, school, play and social settings) over an extended period, in order to provide an appropriate intervention programme that promotes success.

Recognition of a problem

Children, like Matthew, who experience movement learning difficulties are not uncommon at a pre- or Primary School age. Sugden (1984) reinforces this by suggesting that at least 10 per cent of children in mainstream Primary Schools currently experience movement learning difficulty, and they mostly do not receive any help from their teachers, nor are they recognised as having a special educational need of either a short or long-term nature. Rather they are labelled as being physically awkward/clumsy, disorganised, uncoordinated, uncontrolled and lacking physical ability. Brown and Prideaux (1988, p. 187) suggest that:

> Children underfunctioning in movement if given appropriate opportunities, experiences and guidance will enjoy learning in what, at the outset of their school careers, can be a frightening, confusing and threatening curriculum area to cope with.

The capacity of the teacher and parents to act as enablers is a key factor in the child's quest for success in movement learning. The teacher/parents should feel a responsibility to present an environment that is conducive to learning relative to the movement experience and needs of the child, and one in which he can enjoy a sense of trust, security and success. The child should be able to participate freely in the knowledge that his teacher/parents will not create a learning environment which will alienate him as a failure. It may take some children, like Matthew, longer to achieve independence in movement learning, but when a partnership founded on trust and high expectation is cemented, the short and long-term outcomes as a result of the teacher/parent–child combination is exciting and satisfying for all concerned.

A pause for thought

Movement learning development and progress should be the concern of the classteacher and parents, just as is language and number, but to date in most LEA's only significant physical impairment is recognised as requiring concern and provision.

(Brown and Prideaux, 1988, p. 187)

QUESTIONS

1 Discuss whether or not Matthew's underachievement in a movement context could be due to any one or all of the following reasons?
   (i) A lack of understanding of the task
   (ii) A lack of movement experience
   (iii) Aspects in the learning environment that are causing distress
   (iv) A possible physical disability.

2 How could Matthew's underachievement be evident in fine and gross movements?

3 What evidence could there be of Matthew's underachievement in any other aspects of the curriculum?

4 How would you describe Matthew's movement learning behaviour?

5 With what topics, and questions, could you talk to Matthew's parents and gather information on his movement development and experience from birth?

SUPPORTIVE INFORMATION AND MATERIAL

1 Tests

An Infant Teacher's checklist (Gordon and McKinley, 1980, pp. 28–9).
A School Entrant Screening (age 4–5) Coffee Jar Test (Gordon and McKinley, 1980, p. 28).
A Test of Motor Impairment (Stoll, Moyes and Henderson, 1984).

2 Useful reading on movement skill development

BROWN, B. and BAKER, P. (1989) 'A developmental approach to a physical curriculum in a primary area special school', *Bulletin of Physical Education*, 25, 3, 47–9.

GALLAHUE, D.L. (1982) *Understanding Motor Development in Children.* (Chichester: John Wiley and Sons).

GALLAHUE, D.L. (1985) *Developmental Movement Experiences for Children* (London: Collier Macmillan).

HOLLE, B. (1976) *Motor Development in Children: Normal and Retarded* (Oxford: Basil Blackwell).

KEOGH, J. and SUGDEN, D. (1985) *Movement Skill Development* (London: Collier Macmillan).

McCLENEGHAM, B.A. (1978) *Fundamental Movement. A developmental and remedial approach* (Philadelphia: W.B. Saunders).

PAUGRAZI, R.O. (1981) *Movement in Early Childhood and Primary Education* (Minneapolis: Burgess Publishing Co.).

ROBERTSON, M.A. and HALVERSON, L.E. (1984) *Developing Children – their changing movement. A Guide for Teachers* (Philadelphia: Lea and Febiger).

STOTT, D.H., MOYES, F.A. and HENDERSON, S.E. (1984) *Test of Motor Impairment* (Henderson revision) (Harcourt Brace Jovanovich, Footscray High Street, Sidcup, Kent, DA14 5HP).

WICKSTROM, R.L. (1977) *Fundamental Motor Patterns* (Philadelphia: Lea and Febiger).

WILLIAMS, H.G. (1983) *Perceptual and Motor Development* (New Jersey: Prentice-Hall Inc.).

3 Useful reading on movement learning difficulties

BROWN, A. (1987) *Active Games for Children with Movement Problems* (London: Harper and Row).

GORDON, N.C. and McKINLEY, I. (1980) *Helping Clumsy Children* (Edinburgh: Churchill Livingstone).

GORDON, N.C. and McKINLEY, I. (1988) *Children with Neurological Disorders* (Oxford: Blackwell Scientific).

GUBBY, S.S. (1975) *The Clumsy Child* (London: W.B. Saunders and Co. Ltd.).

HASKELL, S., BARRETT, E. and TAYLOR H. (1988) *The Education of Motor and Neurologically Handicapped Children* (London: Croom Helm).

PRICE, R.J. (1980) *Physical Education and the Physically Handicapped Child* (London: Lepus Books).

RUSSELL, J.P. (1987) *Graded Activities for Children with Motor Difficulties* (Cambridge: Cambridge University Press).

TANSLEY, A.E. (1980) *Perceptual Training* (Leeds: E.J. Arnold).

TANSLEY, A.E. (1980) *Motor Education* (Leeds: E.J. Arnold).

UPTON, G. (1979) *Physical and Creative Activities for Mentally Handicapped Children* (Cambridge: Cambridge University Press).

4 Useful reading – journals

ALLONBY, J. (1985) 'Children with Special Educational Needs in Nursery and Reception Classes', *British Journal of Physical Education (BJPE)* Vol. 16, No. 2, March/April, pp. 47–9.

BROWN, A. (1987) 'The Integration of Children with Movement Problems into the Mainstream Games Curriculum', *BJPE* Vol. 18, No. 5, September/October, pp. 230–32.

BROWN, B.A. (1984) 'Adapted Physical Education: Teaching Strategies,' *BJPE* Vol. 15, No. 3 May/June, pp. 76–8.

BROWN, B.A. and PRIDEAUX, R. (1988) 'Children with Movement Learning Difficulties. A Collaborative Initiative with 4–5 year old mainstream children and their parents', *BJPE*, Vol. 19, No. 4, July/October, pp. 186–9.

CUTFORTH, N.J. (1983) 'Self-Concept of the Handicapped Child in Integrated P.E. Settings', *BJPE*, Vol. 14, No. 4, July/August, p. 106.

CUTFORTH, N.J. (1985) 'Physical Education Teachers – A Special Educational Need', *BJPE*, Vol. 16, No. 2, March/April, pp. 62–3.

CUTFORTH, N.J. (1986) 'A Movement Programme for Children with Special Needs in a Comprehensive School', *BJPE*, Vol. 17, no. 2, March/April, pp. 69–70.

CUTFORTH, N.J. (1988) 'The Underachieving Child – Implications for Physical Education', *The Bulletin of Physical Education*, Vol. 24, No. 1, Spring, pp. 16–25.

GALLAGHER, M. (1984) 'Children with Special Needs in the Area of Motor Development', *BJPE*, Vol. 15, No. 3, May/June, pp. 91–3.

GROVES, L. (1985) 'With Whom Shall Children With Special Needs be Physically Educated?', *BJPE*, Vol. 16, No. 1, January/February, pp. 38–9.

HENDERSON, S. (1984) 'The Henderson Revision of the Test of Motor Impairment', *BJPE*, Vol. 15, No. 3 May/June, pp. 72–5.

HIGGINS, B. (1987) 'Building Bridges between Mainstream and Special Schools', *BJPE*, Vol. 18, No. 5, September/October, pp. 221–2.

JORDAN, I. (1987) 'Physical Education for Slow Learners', *BJPE*, Vol. 18, No. 5, September/October, p. 233.

MEEK, G. (1986) 'Awkward performers should not be awkward to teach', *The Bulletin of Physical Education*, Vol. 22, No. 2, Summer, p. 39–41.

MILES, A. and KNIGHT, E. (1987) 'The Contribution of Physical Education to the General Development of Children with Special Educational Needs', *BJPE*, Vol. 18, No. 5, September/October, pp. 204–6.

SUGDEN, D.A. (1984) 'Issues in teaching children with movement problems', *BJPE*, Vol. 15, No. 3, May/June, pp. 68–70.

WILLIAMS, D. (1984) 'Children with Special Needs', *Bulletin of Physical Education*, Vol. 20, No. 2, Summer, pp. 43–5.

WILLIAMSON, D. (1984) 'Student profile and organisational approach to the pupil with Special Needs', *BJPE*, Vol. 15, No. 5, September/October, pp. 128–9.

CASE STUDY 3

Pragna

*The diagnosis and support of a young
child with special needs*

Pragna is the third child born to a non-English speaking mother, and is the only girl with two older brothers, aged four and six years. The family live on the outskirts of a city, father commuting to work. Both brothers are healthy and despite the mother not being able to speak English, the family take full advantage of the medical, educational and recreational activities available, including regular attendance at a Child Health Clinic, taking part in school functions and utilising facilities at a local sports centre.

The mother's care of her children is good. She had an uneventful pregnancy followed by a normal delivery, Pragna's condition at birth was satisfactory and there were no problems during the immediate post-natal period.

Gradual puzzlement led to anxiety about Pragna's later development, and the family sought, and were given, early help from their general practitioner, and the Health Visitor associated with the practice. Through routine health screening the child was found to have a partial hearing loss. This led to referral to, and involvement of, a number of other agencies. Despite the number of other professionals involved, the Health Visitor continued her involvement

---

QUESTIONS

1 Pragna was lucky to have her disability diagnosed at an early stage. Why might she have been unlucky? Do you know of such cases?

2 Rubella in pregnancy is the main cause of sensori-neural deafness. How can health staff help to prevent this?

3 A Health Visitor has no statutory right of entry into the home. Should this be changed? Can state interference be too great?

4 Good liaison between Health Visitor and school is essential to ensure continuity. Is there room for improvement? How?

5 What is required to enable better support to be made available for immigrant families in health education?

6 Is integration a realistic aim for all our children who have special educational needs?

with the family, carrying out routine screening procedures and providing support to the family, even after the child had started school. Only later – as a relationship between the professional and family developed – did the Health Visitor learn that Mrs Patel had contracted rubella (German measles) during the first three months of pregnancy.

SUPPORTIVE INFORMATION AND MATERIAL

1 The Health Visitor's plan of action

(a) The principles of health visiting are the search for health needs, the stimulation of the awareness of health needs, the influence of policies affecting health, and the facilitating of health-enhancing activities. A major role of the Health Visitor is to regularly visit all children under the age of five years commencing when they are 15 days old. All children are regularly seen during the first year of life to carry out a screening programme (which includes a hearing test at seven months).

(b) Pragna's hearing was assessed at seven months at the local health centre using the Sheridan Distraction Test Method. The response on this occasion was poor and, as it is not unusual for a child to fail the first hearing test, a further test was carried out two weeks later. Pragna's response was again poor and she was referred to the local Community Audiology Department for a further hearing assessment. At this stage the mother had reported that Pragna was babbling (although the first language in the family is Punjabi, babbling – the second stage of speech development – would still occur).

(c) Within four weeks of referral to the Audiology Department, Pragna was seen at the local health centre by a Senior Clinical Medical Officer specialising in Audiology. A full hearing assessment was carried out and Pragna was found to have a moderate degree of hearing loss on the right side and a severe loss on the left side. The health visitor was informed of the diagnosis and made immediate contact with the family to provide counselling so that the family could express their feelings about 'knowing that their child was deaf', and to provide explanations, and answers to their questions, about treatment and schooling. They might need help in accepting the disability and encouragement to continue normal family life.

(d) It was necessary then to reassess the needs of the child, and this could include the need for more appropriate stimulation. It was thought that Pragna's educational needs could be met at the local Primary School which had a special needs department. This delighted her parents who were very anxious about the 'stigma' attached to attendance at a special school. The Headmaster and teacher concerned were therefore able to discuss Pragna with the *Health Visitor* who liaises with the school, the *Medical Officer* and the *School Nurse*.

(e) The full plan of action worked out by these staff was thought to be as follows:

(i) Ensure that the family understood the situation and the role of the professionals involved.

(ii) Ensure that Pragna's hearing was maximised with modern hearing aids to allow satisfactory speech development, also ensuring that the family provided appropriate stimulation.

(iii) Liaison between the Health Visitor and other professionals – to ensure consistent approach and advice.

(iv) Ensure that Pragna's name was placed on the Handicapped Register which is held by the Senior District Clinical Medical Officer, so that the child and family receive optimum services which are tailored to the individual need.

(v) Ensure that the services provided are meeting the needs of Pragna and her family by regular monitoring of her development and her family's progress.

(vi) Routine Health Visitor contact includes developmental screening as stipulated by the District Health Authority. This would include a developmental assessment at the ages of nine months and two years.

2 Developmental tests used by a Health Visitor

(a) *Mary Sheridan Stycar Development Sequences* can be used to assess development of mobility, fine movements, language and visual skills. It can be used from birth to five years (for example at 3 months, 9 months and 2 years).

(b) *Denver Developmental Screening Test* is used to assess development in four areas:

(i) Personal/Social – ability to get along with people and take care of oneself.

(ii) Fine motor/adaptive – ability to use the hands and pick up objects and draw.

(iii) Language – ability to hear, follow directions and speak.

(iv) Gross motor – ability to sit, walk and jump.

3 Audiology and the Teacher for the Deaf

(a) Pragna was initially seen at the local health centre by the Senior Clinical Medical Officer (SCMO) specialising in Audiology. A hearing assessment was done using the Sheridan Distraction Test Method. Because Pragna's response was very poor, arrangements were made for Pragna to be seen at the Children's Hearing Assessment Centre (CHAC) for further investigation by the same SCMO.

The teacher for the Deaf was then informed and asked to visit at home. She would also attend the CHAC with the child. At the CHAC further tests were carried out by the SCMO, working with the Audiological Scientist.

Pragna was found to have sensori-neural deafness (loss of 70 decibels) and a conductive loss in the right ear (loss of 40 decibels). Discrimination of speech depends on an ability to hear all phonemes (for example, loss of 40db in high-pitched tones makes unvoiced consonants difficult to detect).

Impressions were taken at this visit for hearing aids. Pragna was also seen by the ENT (Ear Nose and Throat) consultant with a view to surgery which would relieve the catarrh in the right middle ear.

Two weeks after the moulds for hearing aids were taken, Pragna was fitted with hearing aids by the Audiological Scientist and the Teacher for the Deaf. Pragna also continued to be seen at the CHAC at regular intervals to ensure that her hearing was being maximised to allow speech development.

(b)   The Teacher for the Deaf was informed of Pragna's deafness by the SCMO who had carried out the assessment. She made contact with the family and visited the following day. Her role is one of teaching, and demonstrating to parents the skills of language development, and she also acts as a counsellor supporting the parents during the early days after diagnosis. This is essential to ensure that parents are full partners in the management of their child's development

Pragna was visited weekly and during these visits her parents were taught skills to be pursued in the week ahead. As a Teacher for the Deaf she was able to provide essential information on the use and working of the hearing aids.

Pragna and her parents also commenced attending the weekly toy library at a school for children with hearing impairment.

4   Mother and toddler group

Pragna also attended the Mother and Toddler Group near her home, twice a week, thus allowing her to experience interaction with 'normal' children from her neighbourhood.

Mrs Patel did experience difficulties with language at the group, but this was overcome with the help of an aunt (fluent in English) who visited the group frequently with her.

It is the policy of this particular Health Authority to integrate children with special needs into normal pre-school activities in the community as well as mainstream education.

5   ENT consultant

An ENT consultant has regular clinics at the CHAC, thus referrals are made directly to him by the SCMO.

On examination the consultant found Pragna to have no serviceable hearing in the left ear but catarrh was present in the right ear. Pragna's name was placed on the waiting list for urgent adenoidectomy to relieve the catarrh.

6(a)   District handicapped teams

All Health Authorities have District Handicapped Teams which variously includes doctors, nurses, physiotherapists, social workers, and educational psychologists. This team reviews management of the care of all individuals on the register. It also monitors the care given by the Authority, and liaison that takes place between agencies.

6(b)   Handicap register

This is a register of all children with handicaps in a Health District. Some Districts will also include potential handicapping conditions (for example, meningitis and low birth weight). Within Pragna's Health District the register is held in the Community Child Health Department by the SCMO.

The purpose of the register is to help ensure that all children's health, educational, emotional and social needs are met.

By placing Pragna's name on this register, professionals involved are able to meet and discuss their respective roles with, and agree on the future health and educational needs of, the individual and his/her family.

The register facilitates the identification of those children who need specialist assessment and allows Health Authorities to notify the Education Department, in line with the 1981 Education Act, of children who have, or may develop, special educational needs.

After Pragna's fourth birthday a Statement regarding her special educational needs was drawn up as stipulated by the 1981 Education Act.

7   Checklist for Health Visitor after birth of child includes:

MATERNAL FACTORS

Rubella or other viral infection in first 16 weeks of pregnancy
Blood incompatibilities, for example rhesus sensitisation
Hypertension
Diabetes
Other complications of pregnancy

Psychiatric illness in pregnancy
Smoking during pregnancy – ten or more cigarettes per day

PERINATAL

Prolonged or difficult labour
Gestation under 37 weeks
Birth weight under 2500 grammes

POST NATAL

Hyperbilirubinaemia (excessively jaundiced)
Convulsions
Respiratory distress
Congenital abnormalities

GENETIC

Family history of :
deafness
blindness
other.

8 Impairment/disability/handicap

(a) Impairment is the loss or abnormality of psychological, physiological or anatomical structure or function.

(b) Disability is any resulting restriction or lack of ability to perform an activity considered normal.

(c) Handicap is a disadvantage resulting from impairment or disability, which restricts or prevents the fulfilment of a role that is normal (for the age, sex or culture).
(From World Health Organisation's 'Classification of Impairment, Disability and Handicap', 1980.)

9 Useful reading

BLACK, N.A. (1985) 'Glue Ear: The New Dyslexia', *British Medical Journal*, 290, pp. 1963–5.

EWING, I.R. and EWING, A.W.G. (1944) 'The ascertainment of Deafness in Infancy and Early Childhood', *Journal of Laryncology and Ontology*, 59, pp. 309–33.

DAVID, K. and CHARLTON, T. (1987) *The Caring Role of the Primary School* (Basingstoke: Macmillan Education).

DES (1981) *Education Act* (London: HMSO).

DES (1978) *The Warnock Report* (London: HMSO).

LUKER, K. and ORR, J. (1985) *Health Visiting* (Oxford: Blackwell Science Publication).

CETHV (1977) *Principles and Practice of Health Visitors* (London: Council for the Education and Training of Health Visitors).

ROBERTSON, C. (1988) *Health Visiting in Practice* (Edinburgh: Churchill Livingstone).

SHERIDAN, M. (1977) *Children's Developmental Progress* (Windsor: NFER).

CASE STUDY 4

Jeremy

*A change in a Primary School
child's disruptive behaviour*

It is well known within behavioral approaches that differential reinforcement (i.e. positive reinforcement of target behaviours and ignoring of undesired behaviours) is an effective technique for managing classroom behaviour (Presland, 1989). What is less well recognised is that by attending to pupil's misbehaviour (for example, through reprimands, reminders about classroom rules, and ridicule) class teachers may encourage the very behaviours they are attempting to discourage. While teacher behaviours of this type may temporarily halt the misbehaviour, there is a plethora of available evidence showing that the misbehaviour often continues in the long term (Herbert, 1981). Misbehaviour in the classroom, therefore, can be reinforced – albeit unintentionally and unwittingly – through positive reinforcement of undesirable behaviour (Cullinan *et al.*, 1983).

While the following case study is enigmatical in the sense that a variety of reasons could be postulated (yet none could be proved) for the resultant improved behaviour, a plausible explanation is that the behaviour change occurred as a consequence of the presentation of social attention to desired behaviour: however, the ways in which this attention was administered to, and interpreted by, the pupil is not entirely clear and is open to speculation and debate.

Jeremy: a 'damned' nuisance

Jeremy's sixth birthday was only a month away when the classteacher first brought Jeremy's disruptive behaviour to the attention of the Headteacher. During the next several months she complained repeatedly about his aggressive behaviour and frequent temper tantrums (the latter being particularly evident when he could not 'get his own way'). Additionally, Jeremy's behaviour was causing considerable distress to the other children in the class.

When invited to the school the parents were both apologetic and understanding; and confessed that Jeremy's behaviour in the home was often equally distressing. In between bouts of perfectly acceptable behaviour he could be disobedient, rude and destructive. During these misbehaviours the parents were particularly concerned about the safety of the younger sibling, who was three. On one occasion Jeremy had poked him in the eye and the brother had been given emergency treatment at the local hospital.

While the Headteacher felt that Jeremy's school-based problems were not yet of such a serious nature that he should be referred to the Schools' Psychological Service she was well aware that the classteacher needed some specialist support. She decided, therefore, to seek help from a local college lecturer, a psychologist with a particular interest in children's behaviour problems. The lecturer agreed to become involved and met with the Headteacher and classteacher to discuss Jeremy's behaviour.

After this meeting the lecturer requested further information about Jeremy's behaviour both at home and in the classroom. Jeremy's parents were asked to complete Rutter's Behaviour Questionnaire (Child Scale A) and the teacher was asked to record the boy's behaviour on Child Scale B. The RBQ (Rutter *et al.*, 1970) is a widely used screening instrument for identifying children with emotional/behaviour problems. Rutter suggests that children scoring over 14 on scale A and/or over 9 on scale B have problems sufficiently serious to warrant specialist attention. In Jeremy's case the scores obtained from Scale A (=19) and Scale B (=24) indicated that parents and the teacher perceived Jeremy's behaviour problems to be serious. The teacher's description of Jeremy's most serious problems (on Scale B) made reference to his:

> frequent temper tantrums
> frequent fights with other children
> being unliked by his peers, irritable and quick to 'fly off the handle', fussy, and often disobedient
> twitches, and facial tics
> often appearing miserable, and disobedient, and fearful of new situations
> poor concentration and short attention span
> bullying other children.

The parent's questionnaire responses (on Scale A) highlighted the following difficulties in the home:

> temper tantrums
> constant fighting with other children
> solitariness
> irritability
> fear of new situations.

Additional discussion between the lecturer and teachers in the infants school suggested that if Jeremy's on-task behaviour in the classroom could be increased he would have less time available in class during which to produce disruptive behaviour.

The lecturer involved four of his teacher-training students to establish a baseline of Jeremy's on-task behaviour before devising, implementing and evaluating a behaviour modification programme which would reinforce on-task behaviour and ignore (as far as practicable) off-task occasions. Working in pairs – each pair working together on alternate days – the students observed Jeremy's behaviour in the classrooms for ten thirty-minute sessions (i.e. one session each day for two weeks). The students were advised not to interact with the children in the class and to try to mask their observations of Jeremy's behaviour, so far as this was practicable.

Having synchronised their stop-watches at the beginning of each observation period, and working independently, the students observed Jeremy after each sixty seconds and recorded whether he was on-task (working on set work) or off-task. Additionally, on those occasions when Jeremy was not on-task, the students were asked to record the nature of the off-task activity (for example, fighting/temper tantrums).

Results

Average percentage agreements between raters (i.e. an estimation of the agreement between the students' independent observations) were very favourable (91 per cent).

The base-line measure for the two-week period was as follows:

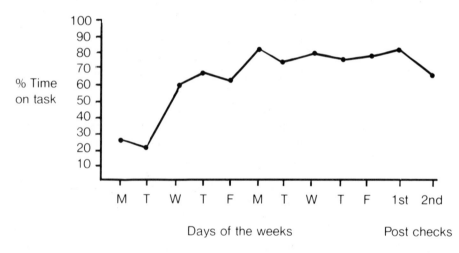

Figure 1

Surprisingly, as can be seen in Figure 1, the students' observations indicated that Jeremy spent increasing periods of time on-task during the two weeks when the observations took place. Furthermore, off task behaviours were only occasionally of a type which interfered with other children in the class. During the last six observation sessions no disruptive behaviours were noted. Follow up enquiries (after one, and then four months) indicated that Jeremy's disruptive behaviour had almost entirely disappeared. On the occasion of the four month check-up obtained Rutter's Behaviour Questionnaire scores were 4 (Scale B) and 8 (Scale A). The teacher RBQ ratings indicated that the misbehaviours noted on the earlier occasion had either disappeared entirely or had been significantly reduced. Furthermore, discussions with the parents revealed that Jeremy's improved behaviour in school had coincided with a similar improvement in the home; they claimed 'he was another person'.

Further talks with the parents failed to identify any change within the home situation which could count for the simultaneous improvements in Jeremy's behaviour in the home and at school.

Conclusion

Two positive outcomes were evident in the above case study. First, while no intervention was planned or implemented, the pupil's behaviour improved during the baseline construction. Second, the school were so delighted with the outcomes that they requested – and were provided with – a series of behaviour modification workshops so that colleagues in the school could become familiar with, and practise, behaviour modification techniques. Nevertheless, to the behavioural scientist the enigma remains; success was apparent – but why?

Case study references

CULLINAN, D., EPSTEIN, M.H. and LLOYD, J.W. (1983) *Behavior Disorders of Children and Adolescents* (New Jersey: Prentice-Hall).

HERBERT, M. (1981) *Behavioural Treatment of Problem Children* (London: Academic Press).

PRESLAND, J. (1989) 'Behavioural Approaches' in T. Charlton and K. David (eds) *Managing Misbehaviour* (Basingstoke: Macmillan Education).

RUTTER, M., TIZARD, J. and WHITMORE, K. (1970) *Education, Health and Behaviour* (London: Longmans).

QUESTIONS

1 What explanations could there be to account for Jeremy's improved behaviour both at school and in the home?

2 Is sufficient emphasis placed upon the development of classroom management skills during initial teacher training?

3 Is it too simplistic to assume that children's behaviour can be managed successfully by systematically administering rewards and punishments?

4 In your experience do schools consult enough with parents when their children's behaviour at school is giving cause for concern? What reasons are there for not doing so?

5 What ethical concerns might teachers (and others) express about the use of behavioural approaches?

SUPPORTIVE INFORMATION AND MATERIAL

1 Behaviour modification

(a) Positive and negative reinforcements

Behavioural approaches make certain assumptions including:

- behaviour is an *observable* and *measurable* response of the child.
- it can be understood in terms of *antecedent* and/or *consequential events*.
- behaviour can be *changed* by altering antecedent and/or consequential events.
- behavioural interventions involve:

    (i)   defining the problem
    (ii) measuring the problem
    (iii) planning/implementing/evaluating the programme.

Key concepts in understanding and changing existing behaviours are those concerned with positive reinforcement and punishment. Neither is a simplistic concept. Charlton and David (1989) remind us that:

- We need to be wary of an overzealous use of reinforcements which may lead to satiation.
- Effort should be reinforced as frequently as actual achievements: by doing so we encourage industry and persistence, without which achievement becomes less likely.
- With some individuals it may be necessary to search hard to find behaviours which warrant praise. Perseverance by the teacher in those instances is often crucial for these may be the very pupils most inclined to misbehave because they have been so infrequently reinforced in the past.
- Reinforcements administered publicly to some pupils may, in fact, be construed as punishment. For a variety of reasons (for example, shyness, and with older ones a fear of ridicule from peers) some pupils dislike having public attention drawn to their efforts and accomplishments. Praise may need to be given privately.
- We are often misled into believing that reinforcements need to be given immediately following the occurrence of desirable behaviour. While this may be true in some instances, when working with the mentally retarded or the very young perhaps, occasions become more frequent with increasing age and maturity when a delay between behaviour and reinforcement may be not only more convenient, but more effective and desirable. Many of the reinforcements we receive as we grow older (such as assessment grades, degree awards and promotion) are often distant from the acts which earned them. As part of the maturing process youngsters need to learn to appreciate and accept this 'time gap'.

- Reinforcements can be signalled in subtle ways, perhaps a wink or a smile. Where applied within large group situations they not only provide variety but can also be used in a 'confidential' manner. While young children may prefer a hug, it is a sad indictment of the age in which we live that we need to be especially guarded about using such contact.
- What is reinforcing (for example, attention and praise) *from one person* may not be so from another. Similarly, what is reinforcing *to one child* may not be so to another. An awareness of these differences gives an indication of the complexity of the reinforcement concept.
- Reinforcements can be given to small and large groups as well as individuals. They can work wonders for group morale.
- On occasions we may need to make clear to pupils what has been reinforced. 'Good' may not necessarily indicate to the pupils 'what is good'. It may be more appropriate and beneficial to comment 'Good. You've worked hard this lesson'.

Negative reinforcements also have a contribution to make to teachers' management of classroom behaviour, but they should be used carefully and sparingly. Whereas positive reinforcers are applied to – and so encourage – good behaviour, negative reinforcers (for example, threats) lead to improved behaviour only because pupils behave appropriately in order to avoid unwanted consequences. An example of negative reinforcement occurs when a teacher informs a class, at the onset of morning break, that they will remain in the classroom until their rowdy behaviour ceases; so to avoid the unpleasant experience of missing some of their break period, the class behaviour has to improve. However, not all children will regard remaining in the classroom as an unpleasant experience!

While negative reinforcers can make useful contributions to teachers' management skills, an over-reliance upon them can result in the frequent use of threats and warnings; conditions that make little, if any, contribution to a healthy classroom ethos, and are inconsistent with good management practices.

(b) Punishments

Similarly they argue that punishment (for example, detention, order-points, extra work, time-out):

- Often serves only to help a behaviour occurring in the future; by itself it does not provide alternative acceptable behaviours which should be used.
- It can generate fears and harmful anxieties which may encourage avoidance behaviours (that is, the pupil may avoid places where, or people from whom, punishment has been – or is – given).
- This avoidance of punishment areas (for example, a particular teacher, subject or classroom) may generalise to other areas (for example, other teachers, subjects, classrooms, school).

- Its application may serve as an unhealthy model for pupils.

Clarizio and McCoy (1983) consider arguments for the use of punishment, and offer the following guidelines for its administration:

- It should not be administered through, or accompanied by, emotive screaming or yelling conveying an attitude of revenge which may, in fact, serve only to reinforce the very misbehaviour which is being punished.
- It should not be too severe.
- Its use over extended periods of time should be avoided. The length and nature of the punishment should match the offence (for example, don't use a sledgehammer to smash a walnut), and the pupil's developmental level.
- The punishment should not take up an inordinate amount of the teacher's time. A detention arranged for after school may be as punishing, if not more so, to the teacher as the pupil.
- Wherever possible, reward related appropriate behaviour either side of the punishment of inappropriate behaviour; thus we reprimand the child when off-task but remember to reward when on-task.
- Whenever possible the pupils should be given a signal warning prior to potential punishment. This, by itself, may deter the misbehaviour. It also provides a degree of fairness where the punishment becomes inevitable (for example, 'You were warned!').
- Research evidence has consistently shown it is usually better to punish early, than to delay until the problem has become magnified.

2 Useful reading

(a) Books

CLARIZIO, H.F. and MCCOY, G.F. (1983) *Behaviour Disorders in Children* (New York: Harper and Row).

CHARLTON, T. and DAVID, K. (1989) *Managing Misbehaviour* (Basingstoke: Macmillan Education).

GRAY, J. and RICHER, J. (1988) *Classroom Responses to Disruption* (Basingstoke: Macmillan Education).

HARROP, A. (1983) *Behaviour Modification in the Classroom* (Sevenoaks: Hodder and Stoughton).

HERBERT, M. (1981) *Behavioural Treatment with Problem Children* (London: Academic Press).

MORGAN, R. (1984) *Behavioural Treatments with Children* (London: Heinemann).

(b) Journals

Mental Handicap – published by the British Institute of Mental Handicap.

Support for Learning – published by The National Association for Remedial Education.

Maladjustment and Therapeutic Education – published by The Association of Workers for Maladjusted Children.

Positive Teaching – published by Positive Teaching Institute, PO Box 45, Cheltenham, Glos., GL5 23BX.

Special Education: Forward Trends – published by The National Council for Special Education.

Links – published by Links Association. Editor – Jean Carlisle, Glenwood, Corntown, Bridgend, Mid Glam.

Educational Psychology – published by the Longman Group, Harlow.

(c) Articles

BROWN, N. and GREEN, Z. (1986) 'Behavioural intervention in a residential special school: a case study', *Maladjustment and Therapeutic Education*, Vol. 4, No. 1, p.36.

BROWN, R. (1985) 'A behavioural approach to helping aggressive children cope in school', *Behavioural Approaches with Children*, Vol 9, No. 3, pp. 79–86.

IMICH, A. and JEFFRIES, K. (1989) 'Management of lunchtime behaviour', *Support for Learning*, 4, 1, 46–52.

MACMILLAN, A. and KOLVIN, I. (1977) 'Behaviour modification in educational settings: a guide for teachers', *Journal of the Association of Workers with Maladjusted Children*, Vol 5, No. 1, pp. 2–18.

REES, P.V. (1986) 'The use of behaviour modification techniques in a comprehensive school', *Maladjustment and Therapeutic Education*, Vol 1, No. 2, pp. 53–62.

WHELDALL, K., BREVANT, K. and SHORTHALL, K. (1986) 'A touch of reinforcement: the effects of contingent teacher touch on the classroom behaviour of young children', *Educational Review*, 38, 3.

James

An eight-year-old boy with dyslexia

James was eight when he was first referred to the Special Needs Advisory and Support Service. The preceding year had been confusing and difficult for him. His parents were divorced, the family home was sold and he, his mother and younger brother moved into a small council house in a nearby town.

   His new school, sympathetic to his changed circumstances, gave him three months to settle but his teachers were puzzled by their conflicting impressions of an intelligent knowledgeable boy only able to read ten words and write four. Assessment and advice were requested.

Initial assessment

(a) 1. The Ravens Progressive Matrices test – a test of non-verbal cognitive ability suggested that he was of good average intelligence.
     2. The British Picture Vocabulary Scale – a test of language acquisition suggested that his verbal ability lay in the low average range.

(b) He identified correctly 14 individual sounds but confused b/d/p/g; and i and j; u and n.

(c) James was left handed, with a dominant left eye, but kicked and led with his right foot. He wears glasses.

(d) He was able to count in ones, twos, fives and tens but was unable to recite tables or remember well-known sequences – for example, the days of the weeks, the months of the year or well-known nursery rhymes.

(e) He had slight articulatory difficulties and problems in saying multi-syllabic words.

(f) His letter formation was poor. Many letters were begun from the wrong position and had the wrong directional flow. The spacing and sizing of letters was erratic and he had already developed 'the left hander's hook'.

(g) There were serious reversal and inversion problems in James' work, with letters, words and numerals.

(h) His teacher described him as 'clumsy in the classroom but superb on the football field'.

(i)   James presented as a quiet, tense and withdrawn child. He avoided eye contact and rarely smiled.

Further assessments

In an effort to explore his learning strategies the advisory teacher carrying out the initial assessment, spent two further sessions with James. He was observed to have significant problems in direction, orientation, sequencing and memory. He wished to learn the word 'bridge', but was still unable to copy the word correctly after four ten-minute sessions. The close juxtaposition of b, d and g confused him and at each attempt one or more letters were reversed, inverted or presented in the wrong order. He became more confident with the tester, established eye contact and smiled.

Parental interview

In discussion with the advisory teacher, the mother told of her concern for James. She reported that:

(a)   Her younger son of four was writing and drawing more easily, had a larger sight vocabulary and was more outgoing than his brother.

(b)   Her husband and his brother had similar literacy problems to those of James. Her father had been diagnosed by his school doctor as 'word blind'.

Recommendations from the Special Needs Advisory and Support Service

(a)   James should have individual help 2½ hours weekly for twelve weeks from an experienced special needs support teacher working in the area team. She would assess more fully his difficulties and plan and begin a remediation programme to be carried out in conjunction with his classteacher.

(b)   The advisory teacher would review his progress in three months.

(c)   The teacher of the hearing impaired working in the special needs advisory team was asked to assess James' hearing.

Response to the programme: further assessment after a period of 12 weeks

(a)   James identified 22 sounds correctly, including b and p.

(b)   The Carver Word Recognition Test – he achieved a score of 5 years 6 months.

(c)   His hearing was found to be within normal limits and his speech discrimination excellent.

(d) There was some improvement in his handwriting, but it remained very immature. He was able to spell 'bridge'.

(e) Mother saw great improvement in his self-esteem. She felt that for the first time he believed that he could learn to read.

(f) To the advisory teacher James said, 'My head is full of stories and I want to write them down'.

(g) In their discussion of James at the completion of the programme, the Special Needs Advisory and Support Service decided that James presented as a child with specific learning difficulties, and his name went forward as a candidate for admission to a unit attached to a mainstream primary school for children with similar problems. He has intensive help for 2½ hours each day by himself or in a group of two, three or four similarly able children. After three months he has settled well into this new school and is more confident and outgoing. He has a sight vocabulary of 40 words and a spelling vocabulary of 20. There will be no miracle cure for James, but with his intense motivation, the support of his parents and a well-structured learning programme at school, it does now seem possible that James will be able to overcome many of his disabilities.

Many of those working in education now prefer the term 'specific learning difficulties' to that of 'dyslexia', highlighting as it does the major characteristic of the group of children to which James belongs – that is that those children experience severe and persistent difficulties in reading and spelling, but are *not* dull children. Their special needs must be met by individual highly structured programmes of work developing through ongoing assessment by the literacy

---

QUESTIONS

1 Where in your area could you obtain information about dyslexia? What use can be made of such material?

2 Why do many teachers and local education authorities still deny its existence?

3 What skills and attitudes should we aim to teach to children with specific learning difficulties?

4 These children best respond to frequent direct teaching of specified skills for short periods of time. How can these time slots be incorporated into our classroom organisation?

5 How can we as teachers ease stress for these children and their parents?

6 In what ways may affective concerns (for example, low self-esteem) influence children's academic development?

tutor. Initial assessment by the specialist will be helpful in formulating the early learning programme, but it will be necessary for the tutor constantly to examine, evaluate and assess the content of that programme and their own teaching style as an understanding of pupils' strengths and weaknesses deepens.

SUPPORTIVE INFORMATION AND MATERIAL

1 Definitions of dyslexia

'A child of average or above average intelligence may be considered to have the disability of dyslexia if he has significant and persistent difficulty with reading, writing and spelling in comparison with his abilities in other spheres, of a degree sufficient to prevent written work reflecting his true ability and knowledge in spite of adequate teaching.'
(Medical and Health Services Sub-committee of the British Dyslexia Association)

'A disorder in children, who, despite conventional classroom experience, fail to achieve the language skills of reading, writing and spelling commensurate with their intellectual abilities.'
(World Federation of Neurologists of which Dr Macdonald Critchley, leading
world authority on dyslexia was President).

'A specific language difficulty mainly concerned with the nitty gritty of words and letters.'

(Dr Margaret Newton, Aston University)

2 Information and material may be obtained from:

The British Dyslexia Association,
98 London Road,
Reading,
RG1 5AU
Telephone 0734 668271

The Dyslexia Institute,
133 Gresham Road,
Staines,
Middlesex, TW18 2AJ.
Telephone 0784 463935

The Dyslexia Centre,
Tavistock House (South),
Tavistock Square,
London, WC1A 9LB

Helen Arkell Dyslexia Centre,
14 Crondale Road,
London, SW6 4BB.

3 Publishers specialising in materials for children with specific learning difficulties include:

Better Books,
15a Chelsea Road,
Lower Weston,
Bath.
Telephone 0225 28010

Learning Development Aids,
Duke Street,
Wisbech,
Cambs., PE13 2AE.

4 Useful games

Games, as part of a structured programme, provide multi-sensory experiences and repetitive practice to enable children to acquire particular reading and spelling skills. Many familiar games can be used in their original form or can be adapted to suit the particular needs of an individual child. The following are examples of collections of games and thematic materials that include games.

The Aston Portfolio
Stile Materials
Unique Reading Games –all available
   from
Learning Development Aids,
Park Works,
Norwich Road,
Wisbech, Cambs., PE13 2AX.

Sharp Eye –
A thematic learning programme.
Ginn,
Prebendal House,
Parson's Tce,
Aylesbury,
Bucks., HP20 2QZ.

5 Books that list useful resources including games

SCHOLASTIC PUBLICATIONS LTD. (1987) *Bright Ideas – Teacher handbooks: a) Reading, b) Spelling, c) Developing Children's Writing* (Marlborough House, Holly Walk, Leamington Spa, CV32 4LS).

CRIVELLI, V. (1986) *The SLD Handbook and index* (The County Council of Hereford and Worcester).

HERBERT, D. and DAVIES-JONES, G. (1984) *A Classroom Index of Phonic Resources* (Stafford: NARE Publications).

BARRY, J., FERGUSON, C., MCWHORTER, K. and WALKER, A. (1978) *Hip Pocket Book of Games* (London: Harcourt Brace Jovanovich).

THOMSON, M. (1986) *Word Quest* (Learning Development Aids, Wisbech, Cambs., PE13 2AX).

THOMSON, M. (1989) *The Book of Letters* (Learning Development Aids, Wisbech, Cambs., PE13 2AX).

6 Useful addresses

Advisory Centre for Education,
18 Victoria Park Square,
London, E2 9PB.
Telephone 081 980 4596

Voluntary Organisation, Communication and Language,
336 Brixton Road,
London, SW9.
Telephone 071 274 4029

Parents Advice Line (run by the magazine *Special Children*)
Box 161,
Rode,
Bath.
Telephone 0898 333001

Dyslexia Institute,
133 Gresham Road,
Staines, TW18 2AJ.

Gifted Children's Information Service,
941 Warwick Road,
Solihull.

National Association for Remedial Education,
2 Lichfield Road,
Stafford, ST17 4JX.
Telephone 0785 46872

United Kingdom Reading Association (UKRA),
Hon. Information Officer,
Rubicon,
20 Crane Drive,
Verwood,
Wimborne,
Dorset.

NATLIC (National Association of Teachers of Language Impaired

2 Vernon Close,
St Peter's Field,
Mantley,
Worcs, WR6 6QY

7 Test materials

The following tests are available to teachers and are designed to aid in the identification of specific learning difficulties.

MILES, T.R. *The Bangor Dyslexia Test* (for pupils 6–13 years). Learning Development Aids, Park Works, Norwich Road, Wisbech, Cambs., PE13 2AX.

NEWTON, M. and THOMPSON, M. *The Aston Index* (for pupils 5–14 years). Learning Development Aids, Park Works, Norwich Road, Wisbech, Cambs., PE13 2AX.

Other tests referred to in the case study are:

CARVER, C. (1984) *Word Recognition* (test for 4–8½ years). Edward Arnold, Hodder and Stoughton, PO Box 702, Mill Road, Dunton Green, Sevenoaks, Kent, TN13 2YD.

DUNN, L. M. and WHETTON, C. (1982) *The British Picture Vocabulary Scale – a test of language acquisition* (for pupils 2½–18 years). (Windsor: NFER–Nelson).

ROWAN, J.C. *Rowans Progressive Matrices – a test of non-verbal cognitive ability* (standard 6–10, advanced 11 upwards).

8 Useful reading

BRADLEY, L. (1986) *Poor speller, poor reader: understanding the problem* (Reading and Language Information Centre, University of Reading).

BRANWHITE, T. (1986) *Designing Special Programmes* (London: Methuen).

BRYANT, P. and BRADLEY, L. (1985) *Children's Reading Problems, Psychology and Education* (Oxford: Blackwell).

CHARLTON, T. (1986) 'Reading Difficulties: effect of therapeutic interventions', *Links*, 12, 1, 23–7.

COTTERELL, G. (1985) *Teaching the Non-Reading Dyslexic Child* (Learning Development Aids).

COTTERELL, G. (1975) *Diagnosis in the Classroom* (Reading and Language Information Centre, University of Reading).

COWDERY, L. *et al.* (1984) *Teaching Reading through Spelling: 1. Resource Book – Diagnosis. 2. Resource Book – The Foundations of the Programme* (Kingston Polytechnic).

CRIVELLI, V. (1986) *The S.L.D. Handbook and Index* (Useful list of resources) (County Council, Hereford and Worcester).

ELLIS, A. (1984) *Reading, Writing and Dyslexia* (Hilsdale, NJ: Hemel Hempstead: Lawrence Erlbaum).

HORNSBY, B. and SHEAR, F. (revised) (1980) *Alpha to Omega* (London: Heinemann).

LAMBLEY, H. (1989) 'Learning and Behaviour Problems' in Charlton, T. and David, K. (eds) *Managing Misbehaviour* (London: Macmillan Education).

NAIDOO, S. (1972) *Specific Dyslexia* (London: Pitman).

SNOWLING, M. (1985) *Children's Written Language Difficulties* (Windsor: NFER Nelson).

SNOWLING, M. (1987) *Dyslexia-Cognitive Developmental Perspectives* (Oxford: Blackwell).

LAWRENCE, D. (1985) 'Improving self-esteem and reading', *Educational Research*, 27, 3, 194–7.

Patrick

Possible child abuse

One of the most onerous responsibilities of the class teacher is to be vigilant for, and appropriately responsive to, the recognition of signs and symptoms suggesting possible child abuse. However, some teachers have not been equipped with adequate pre- or in-service training in areas associated with the recognition of these signs and symptoms, and the referral procedures associated with them. When the concerns of the teacher are aroused they are likely to be confronted with the perplexing dilemma about whether or not to share their concerns with others.

This case study is concerned with this type of dilemma. While there is no conclusive ending to the study, the contents of the Supportive Information and Material section includes information intended to prove helpful to colleagues confronted with similar predicaments.

Patrick was a slight and withdrawn boy. During his four years at Broadside Primary School he had remained remarkably inconspicuous. His behaviour was never troublesome, and his teacher commented that his work appeared neither sufficiently good nor bad to warrant additional attention from her! For all intents and purposes, Patrick appeared almost 'faceless', someone who did not draw attention to himself, and never became prominent – socially or academically – in the classroom (or elsewhere in the school). Until the incidents mentioned later, he had never given discernible reasons for any of the teachers to generate any concerns on his behalf.

It was only upon a detailed reflection by staff that anomalies began to surface. First, no member of staff could recollect ever seeing either of Patrick's parents. Indeed, there was no record of his parents ever visiting the school either on Parents' Evenings, or on any other formal or social occasions. Second, teachers failed to recollect any instance during which the boy had talked about his home, holidays, or outings. Additionally, he appeared to have no member of his class with whom he was particularly friendly, although there was no evidence of his being ostracised, or teased, by his peers.

This staff 'reflection' had been instigated by the Headteacher during a cold December morning after Patrick's teacher had sought advice from the Head during the morning breaktime. The teacher, Mrs Lewis, came to the Headteacher's office because of incidents which had caused her great concern. She recounted how a few weeks earlier she had noticed marks on Patrick's face. In addition to a black eye he had extensive lacerations on his cheeks and forehead. Her enquires elicited mumbles that he had fallen off his bicycle. On that occasion, and quite understandably, Mrs Lewis saw no reason to take the matter further. On a subsequent occasion – a few weeks later, on the December morning in question – she observed further injuries which did arouse her concern. While changing for PE she had noticed weals across Patrick's back. When she had taken him to one side and asked him how this had happened, he began crying. Further attempts by her to investigate the cause of the injuries were futile. Finally, she had told him to get dressed. She then took him in the hall with her, where he read a book while the others continued with their PE lesson. When breaktime was signalled she asked Patrick if he would tidy the class library for her. She then left to see the Headteacher.

Was there, she asked the Headteacher, reason to think that Patrick had been abused at home?

QUESTIONS

1 Faced with this situation do you think the teacher's reaction was a reasonable one?

2 If the Headteacher shared the teacher's concern what could (should) his next action(s) be?

3 How much knowledge and understanding of the signs and symptoms of child abuse have you received during your training?

4 Where could you obtain information on the signs and symptoms of child abuse?

5 Discuss possible 'signs and symptoms' of the four major categories of child abuse.

SUPPORTIVE INFORMATION AND MATERIAL

1 Useful addresses

National Society for the Prevention of Cruelty to Children,
67 Saffron Hill,
London, EC1N 8RS.
Telephone 071 242 1626

Child Abuse Training Unit
National Children's Bureau,
8 Wakley Street,
London EC1V 7QE.
Telephone 071 278 9441

Childline,
Faraday Building,
Queen Victoria Street,
London EC4 4BU.
Telephone Admin. 071 336 2380;
Children's Counselling 0800 1111

OPUS (Organisation for Parents Under Stress),
106 Godstone Road,
Whyteleafe,
Surrey CR3 06B.

Barnardo's,
Tanners Lane,
Barkingside,
Essex 1G6 1QG.
Telephone 081 550 8822

End Physical Punishment of Children (EPOCH),
77 Holloway Road,
London N7 8JZ.
Telephone 071 700 0627

2 Types of abuse

The NSPCC document 'How the N.S.P.C.C. Works' lists the following types of child abuse:

(a) Physical abuse

(b) Sexual abuse

(c) Emotional abuse

(d) Neglect

(See section 3 for behavioural/physical/social indicators of possible abuse).

3 Indications of possible abuse

LEA and NSPCC documents provide detailed indications of possible child abuse. Circular 4/88 (DES) comments that:

> Because they are in regular contact with children, school staff are particularly well placed to observe outward signs of abuse, or unexplained changes in behaviour or performance which may indicate abuse. Bruises, lacerations and burns may be apparent, particularly when children change their clothes for physical education and sports activities. Possible indicators of physical neglect, such as inadequate clothing, poor growth, hunger or apparently deficient nutrition, and of emotional neglect, such as excessive dependence or attention-seeking, may be noticeable. Sexual abuse may indicate physical signs, or lead to substantial behavioural change including precocity or withdrawal. These signs and others can do no more than give rise to suspicion – they are not in themselves proof that abuse has occurred. But as part of their pastoral responsibilities teachers should be alert to all such signs.

More specifically, the NSPCC in their publication 'Protecting Children: A guide for Teachers on Child Abuse' (p.6) lists a number of behavioural signs which may help alert the teacher to cases of suspected abuse including:

- repeated minor physical injuries (for example, bruising, cuts etc.)
- children who are dirty, smelly, poorly clothed or who appear underfed
- children who have lingering illnesses which are not attended to
- deterioration in school work or significant changes in behaviour without explanation
- aggressive behaviour, severe tantrums
- an air of 'detachment' or 'don't care' attitude
- overly compliant behaviour, 'watchful' attitude
- sexually explicit behaviour (for example, playing games and showing awareness which is inappropriate for the child's age)
- continual open masturbation, aggressive and inappropriate sex play
- the child who is reluctant to go home or is kept away from school by a parent
- does not join in school social activities, has few school friends
- does not trust adults, particularly those who are close
- 'tummy pains' with no medical reason
- eating problems, including over-eating, loss of appetite
- disturbed sleep, nightmares, bedwetting
- running away from home, suicide attempts, self-inflicted wounds
- reverting to younger behaviour, depression, withdrawal
- relationships between the child and adults which are secretive and exclude others.

4   Responsibilities and procedures

(a)   The Child Care Act (1980) provides the local authority with a duty to make available such advice, guidance and assistance as promote the welfare of children by diminishing the need to receive them into care, to keep them in care or bring them before the Juvenile Court.

(b)   Local Authorities all have their own written procedures on Child Abuse which they make available to professionals working with children. In addition to the inclusion of 'indicators of child abuse' they also include information for the guidance of schools when a suspected case of child abuse is encountered. Normally, these procedures involve (see DES Circular 4/88 and LEA documentation):

(i)   reporting the case immediately to:

(a)   the Social Services Team Manager

(b)   the Area Education Welfare Officer

(c)   the District Senior Clinical Medical Officer so that arrangements can be made for the child to be examined by a doctor.

(ii)   where sex abuse is suspected then the Headteacher – or designated senior member of staff who holds the responsibility for co-ordinating the school's response to child abuse – must telephone immediately the Social Services Team Manager so that a multi-disciplinary approach can be arranged (i.e. involving Social Services/Health Authority/Police). Usually, this telephone referral must be followed by a written report from the school.

(iii) the Headteacher advising parents when a medical examination shall take place; parents are invited to attend the medical inspection but the examination will take place if parents are unwilling to attend.

(iv) the Headteacher, and nominated teachers from the school, attending all subsequent Case Conferences.

5 Cleveland Inquiry: a salient reminder!

In the introduction to the Children Society's special publication (1989) entitled *Responses to Cleveland. Improving Services for Child Sexual Abuse* Peter Riches comments:

> In years to come the Cleveland Inquiry will be remembered not so much for blaming individual or agency responses, not for making recommendations to improve practice and the law, but rather as the point at which it became official that the sexual abuse of children takes place on a wide scale.

(p.1)

6 Estimates of child abuse

Research findings often appear contradictory; some give far higher incidence levels than others. What appears to be widely accepted is that while we have no definitive idea of the extent of the various forms of abuse, official figures such as those issued by the NSPCC are unlikely to provide a true estimate of the number of children who are abused. Many cases, for a number of reasons, go unreported.

(a) Peter Maher (1988) cites research enquiries which indicate that some one in ten of children are, or have been, the subject of some form of child *sex abuse*. He refers to another study which suggests that the rate may be as high as one in three. Official figures such as those given by the NSPCC are unlikely to provide helpful data in terms of the incidence of such abuse – and may seriously underestimate the true extent of abuse. For every case reported there may be many others which go unreported. How many we still do not know.

(b) A Mori Poll conducted by Baker and Duncan in 1985 interviewed 2019 adults. In this sample 12 per cent of women and 8 per cent of men reported that they had been sexually abused as children.

(c) NSPCC figures:
  (i) Referrals in 1987/88 – 21 325
        Children involved – 42 853
        Children helped – 48 070.
  (ii) 37 per cent of referrals involved children under the age of five years
        66 per cent of referrals involved children aged nine years or under
        84 per cent of referrals involved children aged fourteen years or under.
  (iii) 55 per cent of referrals came from the general public
        18 per cent of referrals came from parents
        16 per cent of referrals came from public officials
        10 per cent of referrals came from other relatives
        1 per cent of referrals came from the child.

(d) 8000 calls a day are made to Childline.

(e) 50 – 75 per cent of abusers are fathers or father figures (see NSPCC *Research Briefing No 9*, 1987).

(f) The American Humane Association (1984) reports that there were 929 310 substantiated cases of child abuse in the USA during 1982.

7 The teacher's role

Maher (1988) comments that there will never be an understanding or acceptance of the importance of the teacher's role in detecting, and helping, pupils who are being abused as long as teachers contend that:

> this is not a major problem and the numbers of abused children that I come into contact with is small   (p.282)

In the same publication (p. 286) he argues for the following three levels of training for teachers:

(a) Awareness training for all staff in schools, including teachers so that they can begin to understand the nature of the problem and their role in it. They need as well to understand how to react and who to tell. They need to understand how their school procedure works and who has responsibility.

(b) Headteachers, and all senior staff in larger schools, need that initial level of training, but also more detailed input on legal responsibilities, how to establish and review effective school procedures, how the local education authority (LEA) guidelines operate, how to deal appropriately with parents and children and how the multi-professional network operates.

(c) Nominated 'child abuse teacher contacts', first recommended by Louis Blom-Cooper (London Borough of Brent, 1985), whose role would be to simplify the relationships between schools and other professional and voluntary bodies dealing with abuse cases, need much more extensive training. They certainly need the level of training suggested above for Headteachers, but this should be carried forward one further step. The need for close links within a multi-professional working environment, would be facilitated by joint training programmes. It is at this level that multi-professional training must be afforded and such training is crucial to the effectiveness of these teachers.

8   Considerations for parents (and in some instances, teachers)

The NSPCC pamphlet 'Putting Children First' contains a number of statements which adults would do well to acknowledge (yet occasionally don't), including:

- Children are not mini-adults. They see and experience the world differently to adults.
- Babies learn language mainly from their parents speaking to them.
- Apart from body language, crying is a baby's only language.
- Parents describe 'falling in love' with their babies. 'Bonding' is essential for babies, but neither immediate nor automatic for parents.
- Babies and young children have no notion of your needs.
- When a toddler is 'clingy' it is because you are the most important person in her/his life. Sooner or later s/he will mix with others.
- A young child up to two or so cannot be 'naughty' because s/he does not mean to do anything wrong. S/he can be very annoying though.
- Play for a child is not just passing the time – it is a way of practising skills and learning about the world and people in it.
- Two-year-olds do not understand 'mine' or 'yours', but think the whole world is there to please them.
- All small children are aggressive. Gentle persuasion is needed rather than aggression from you, which simply confirms that big people hit little people.
- Many children do not realise that they have a right to say no to unwanted touching of their bodies.
- Children do not fully understand a right from wrong until they are about seven and do not have a 'conscience'. In 'moral matters' therefore *example* is more important than words to young children though gentle praise never goes amiss.
- Between the ages of 9–12 children will begin to understand social injustice and unfair treatment. They realise, for example, that lies are bad whereas a younger child knows that it is wrong to lie but will not understand why.
- Young children are likely to see the break up of a relationship as their fault.
- Adolescents need guidance, support and 'example'.
- Adolescents get information about sex from somewhere. It is best if it is

from you. At the very least it helps if parents acknowledge the need and check the information is accurate.

9 The Children Act (received Royal Assent on 16 November 1989)

(a) The Health Minister, David Mellor, contends that the Act will improve the ability to protect children from harm. Some of the major changes in legislation, resulting from the Act, include:

(i) the introduction of an Emergency Protection Order (EPO) to replace the Place of Safety Order (PSO). The EPO will have a duration of only eight days, but can be extended by a further seven days (compared to the twenty-eight days of the PSO). The police will be able to take the child into their protection for up to 72 hours if they believe that the child would otherwise be exposed to significant harm.

(ii) the introduction of an Education Supervision Order to replace Care Orders where a child of compulsory school age is not being properly educated, through poor attendance.

(iii) Additionally there will be a continuing use of Care and Supervision Orders when a child has suffered significant harm, or is likely to suffer such harm. Interim Care Orders will also be available where proceedings have been adjourned or where courts have been asked to investigate. They will, however, be available for a period of only eight weeks initially (unlike the arrangements prior to the Act, where they could be reviewed automatically).

(b) While presenting the Children Bill to the House of Lords (December 1988) the Lord Chancellor commented that:

The Bill in my view represents the most comprehensive and far reaching reform of child care law which has come before Parliament in living memory

(c) David Mellor later remarked that the Act replaced legislation which was 'confusing, piecemeal, outdated, often unfair and, in important respects, ineffective'.

(d) In his Report to the National Children's Bureau AGM (1989) the NCB Director, Dr Ronald Davie, drew attention to the Act's emphasis upon:

. . . the principle that the upbringing of children is primarily the responsibility of parents. For example, even if the grounds for a care order are proved, it is now necessary also to be satisfied that making an order is better for the child than not making an order (and thus leaving him/her within the family). A second example of this principle is that the new Emergency Protection Order, replacing the old Place of Safety Order, can be used, 'if, but only if, . . . there is reasonable cause to believe that the child is likely to suffer significant harm.' Furthermore, as many will know, the new order can last no more than eight days and can only be extended once, for a period of seven days. Thirdly, working in partnership with parents is now required of professionals by law and is no longer simply a matter of good practice.

10 Useful publications

(i) Books, articles, pamphlets

BRENT, London Borough of (1985) *A Child in Trust* (London: London Borough of Brent).

MILNER, A. and BLYTH, E. (1988) *Coping with Child Sexual Abuse: A Guide for Teachers* (London: Longman).

RICHES, P. (1989) 'Responses to Cleveland: Improving Services for Child Sexual Abuse', *Children and Society, Special Publication* (London: Whiting and Birch Ltd.).

MAHER, P. (1987) *Child Abuse: The Educational Perspective* (Oxford: Blackwell).

MAHER, P. (1988) 'Lessons for Teachers from Cleveland. More Questions than Answers.' *Children Society*, 2, 3, 279–88.

DES (1988) *Working Together for the Protection of Children from Abuse: Procedures within the Education Services*, DES Circular 4/88 (A copy of this document should be available to teachers in all schools).

RUSSELL, D.E.H. (1983) 'The incidence and prevalence of intra familial and extra familial sexual abuse of female children', *Child Abuse and Neglect*, 7 (2).

BUTLER-SLOSS, RT HON JUSTICE E. (1988) *Report of the Inquiry into Child Abuse in Cleveland 1987* (London: HMSO).

KIERNAN, C. (1988) 'Child Abuse: A case for change?' *British Journal of Special Education*, 15, 4, 140–52.

MOORE, J. (1985) *The ABC of Child Abuse Work* (Gower).

ROGERS, W., HEVEY, D. and ASH, E. (1989) *Child Abuse and Neglect: Facing the Challenge*. (Open University/Batsford).

The NSPCC produce a number of useful publications including:

Putting Children First. Describes the NSPCC 'Putting Children First' Campaign 1988–9.

How the N.S.P.C.C. Works. Provides information on the history of the NSPCC, the training of its staff, how the organisation is financed and the children it has helped.

Protect Your Child. This is a guide about child abuse for parents. Of the

50 629 children the NSPCC helped in 1986/87 nearly one-fifth were referred by parents themselves.

The Forgotten Children. Discusses why parents may neglect their children/ attempts to help readers understand what it is like to be neglected/ refers to the law and how it addresses child neglect/ makes reference to ways in which the NSPCC seeks to help these children/ lists some signs and symptoms of neglect.

Protecting Children: A Guide for Teachers on Child Abuse. Contains invaluable information for teachers. Its contents includes information on:

(a) identifying child abuse
(b) responding to children
(c) listening and talking to children
(d) working with parents
(e) the investigation
(f) getting support.

(Copies of NSPCC publications are obtainable from the Headley Library, 67 Saffron Hill, London EC1N 8RS. Telephone 071 242 1626).

(ii) Training Packs

Many are now available, but these are among the more recent publications. Further information on such materials can be obtained from the Child Abuse Training Unit at the National Children's Bureau, 8 Wakly Street, London EC1V 7QE (Telephone 071 278 9441).

(a) Open University (P554) *Child Abuse and Neglect: An Introduction*.

(b) *Responding to Child Abuse*. A pack for teachers, parents and other relevant agencies. Produced by Community Education Development Centre. Available from CEDC, Briton Rd., Coventry CV4 2LF (Telephone 0203 440814).

(c) Children's Society. *Working with Sexually Abused Children*. Available from Children's Society, Edward Rudolph House, Margaery Street, London WC1X 0JC (Telephone 071 837 4299).

(d) The Children's Society have published three brief and very useful brochures on *Running Away* aimed at teachers, parents and pupils.

CASE STUDY 7

Sally

An epileptic person fit for work

Sally was born perfectly healthy, but was tragically involved in a road traffic accident near her house at the age of six. She sustained internal injuries, resulting in the removal of her spleen, and brain damage resulting in epilepsy. She was the second of a family of four, up to that time living a normal existence.

When she had recovered enough for a decision to be made on her subsequent school life, there was a certain pressure to seek special rather than mainstream education because of the dual impairment. This was resisted by her mother whose wish was to integrate her as much as possible. The school, which was small and caring, agreed, and so she was educated with her peers from the age of seven to the age of eleven. However by the age of eleven her epileptic attacks had not diminished although drug therapy was given, and there was a large question mark over her transfer to the local comprehensive school, an eleven to sixteen school in a mixed catchment area, where it was feared that her condition might not be as well managed as in the junior school.

A case conference was called with the Child Guidance Service Psychologist, the doctor, the mother and the Headmaster, where it was decided that the school could, with good will, manage the epilepsy. It was pointed out at this time to the mother that either through medication or through cerebral damage there was a deficit in intellectual ability. It was decided at this time that a pastoral tutor would be a teacher who had had personal experience of impairment at first hand from his own daughter. He and the mother drew up ground rules for any fits, and how the interpersonal side of relations between Sally and her peer group should be managed. About this time Sally's father left home, unable to cope with the strain of caring, and his wife's assumed over-protectiveness. The family moved from the owner-occupied house to an older municipally rented house near the school. The family were dependent on social security and rent rebate, for Sally's mother with two younger children and a disabled daughter was unable to work at a wage high enough to compensate her for loss of social benefits.

When Sally became fifteen there was another series of choices. The careers officer serving the school, after having seen Sally and her mother once, decided that the case required the resources of the specialist careers officer dealing with special needs, on the ground that he had more time and more expertise in solving these problems and was skilled in parent/child counselling.

A case conference was called between Sally, her mother, the pastoral tutor and the specialist careers officer, in which it was decided that:

(a)   Sally was to sample work in open employment conditions with the specialist careers officer holding a watching brief;

(b)   Sally's medical condition and the practical limitations be divulged to the employer, and that the specialist careers officer be responsible for this action;

(c)   Sally's mother was to be kept fully informed, and invited to the employer's premises;

(d)   the school, through the pastoral tutor, be responsible for a full academic and social report where necessary to the employer.

An employer, who was keen to help and well known to the specialist careers officer, was contacted and an interview set up. This employer had employed people with disabilities before and was sympathetic in a real and practical way. He designed and manufactured children's dresses. Sally's job was to be a trainee machinist, on a six-month period of assessment to see whether she could attain her target. There were no qualms over her epilepsy. The employer was aware of the full facts, and had experience of people with epilepsy, knew that almost all have warnings, and those affected tend to fall backwards rather than into the machine. She started well but slowly, but unfortunately after the six-month period could not 'make her money'. It is an important principle that a person who is impaired ought not to be an object of charity, but should be able to earn his or her own 'corn'. On the positive side Sally's time keeping, her conscientious attitude, and above all her management of her own epilepsy had convinced her that she wanted to work rather than live on social benefits. Moreover, it had convinced Sally's mother that there was little to worry about. The experience gained and the reference from the first employer enabled the specialist careers officer to place her in another company (making socks for Marks and Spencer) as an inspector, a responsible job if one knows the sales and marketing policy of that company. The job lasted three years until the line was changed and retraining became necessary. Sally did not retrain successfully and has been at the same firm ever since on inspection and packing of fashion knitwear.

QUESTIONS

1 What qualities are needed in a person taking self-medication? How can schools help a person develop such qualities?

2 How can schools develop an awareness of the difficulties faced by teachers and the peer group in coming into contact with children and young adults with epilepsy?

3 'People with epilepsy suffer a dual disability – fits, and the prejudice of the society in which they live whether at school or in employment.' Can you think of measures which will reduce this?

4 The choice of career is a personal one and nothing to do with the family or outside 'experts'. Can this argument be sustained in the case of any school leaver, whether impaired or not?

SUPPORTIVE INFORMATION AND MATERIAL

1 Types of epilepsy

The most useful definition of Epilepsy is 'an upset in the electrical activity of the brain'. These can be:

(a) Tonic – a general stiffening of the muscles without rhythmical jerking which results in a collapse to the ground.

(b) Atonic – a sudden loss of muscle tone which results in a collapse to the ground.

(c) Mynoclonic – abrupt jerking of the limbs with or without loss of consciousness.

(d) Absences – in which there is a brief interruption of consciousness without any other signs, except for a fluttering of the eyelids. (Commonly called petit mal.)

(e) Partial Fits – a disturbance of brain activity in a distinct area of the brain. These are known as 'focal' and are not to be confused with petit mal. Consciousness is not impaired and the fit is confined to one limb or part of a limb, or to unusual sensations such as pins and needles in a distinct part of the body. Complex partial fits would affect the parts of the brain controlling mood and emotion.

2 Helping organisations

British Epilepsy Association,
Crowthorne House,
New Wokingham Road,
Wokingham,
Berkshire, RG11 3AY.

National Society for Epilepsy,
Chalfont Centre for Epilepsy,
Gerrards Cross,
Bucks, SL9 0RJ.

There are in most large towns local self-help groups. Refer to your local charities directory, or write to the British Epilepsy Association asking to be put in touch (See section 6 for further addresses).

3   A teacher's guide to epilepsy

(a)   Cushion the pupil's head with something soft.

(b)   Do NOT try to put anything between the teeth or give anything to drink.

(c)   Loosen with care any tight clothing around the neck.

(d)   Do NOT call a doctor or ambulance unless fits follow one another without the child regaining consciousness.

(e)   After convulsion has ceased, turn child on his/her side, in a semi-prone position to aid breathing and general recovery, and if possible stay with the child to offer reassurance during the confused period.

4   Critical comments from a person with epilepsy

(a)   A number of *jobs* are not open to epileptics, because of the problems of insurance. An epileptic would not normally be able to get employment on a building site, for example.

(b)   Some *sports and pastimes* may be actually barred by law, anything that could endanger your life or the lives of others. People with epilepsy *may* not be allowed to hold a driving licence. The current regulations allow a licence to be granted if an applicant with epilepsy satisfies the following conditions:

They shall have been free from any epileptic attack during the period of 2 years immediately preceding the date when the licence is to have effect; or

In the case of an applicant who has had such attacks only whilst asleep during a period of at least 3 years preceding the date when the licence is to have effect;

AND in both cases

the driving of a vehicle by the applicant is not likely to be a source of danger to the public.

Additionally the law prevents anybody who has experienced an epileptic attack since the age of five years old driving a Heavy Goods Vehicle or Public Service Vehicle.

(c)   There is also the position of someone who holds a driving licence, and becomes affected later in life. Because of medical ethics, the doctor cannot inform the licensing authorities, so the authorities are totally dependent on the affected person being honest, to inform them. There is the case of a service engineer developing epilepsy who had been earning £150 per week at the time, who dropped £25 per week on the dole with a radical alteration in living standards, received very little in way of state benefits, and experienced the need to move home to where his wife could gain better employment. There was a loss of self-esteem, confidence and a reversal of roles within the marriage.

(d)   This, of course, means that the job implications are far more limited than is at first apparent – relying on public transport or generosity of workmates, friends, and family.

(e)   Even if the epilepsy is 'controlled' by drugs, all forms of personal insurance (for example, driving, life, medical) are much more expensive than normal.

(f)   The public at large contrive to regard epilepsy as an illness and the epileptic is constantly asked – 'Do you feel alright? Have you got over it now?' I personally ended up feeling and thinking, after I had been asked these questions for what seemed the millionth time, that 'the next person to ask me that, is going to get one straight in the chops.' It was almost as though people were determined that I should not forget that they thought I was ill/disabled. The biggest problem is being prevented from doing things that you know you can do, but because of the problem (even when it is controlled) are not permitted to do.

5   Useful leaflets, obtainable from:

British Epilepsy Association,
Anstey House,
40 Hanover Square,
Leeds,
West Yorkshire, LS3 1BE.
Telephone (0532) 439393

(a)   Epilepsy and Driving
(b)   The child with Epilepsy
(c)   Television Epilepsy
(d)   Mothers with Epilepsy

6   British Epilepsy Association regional offices are located at:

Northern Ireland:
The Old Postgraduate Medical Centre,
Belfast City Hospital,
Lisburn Road,
Belfast, BT9 7AB.
Telephone Belfast (0232) 248414

Northern Region:
313 Chapeltown Road,
Leeds,
W. Yorks, LS7 3JT.
Telephone Leeds (0532) 621076

Midland Region:
Room No. 1,
First Floor,
Guildhall Buildings,
Navigation Street,
Birmingham, B2 4BT.
Telephone Birmingham (021) 643 7524

Epilepsy Wales – (Epilepsi Cymru):
142 Whitchurch Road,
Cardiff, CF4 3NB.
Telephone Cardiff (0222) 628744

South East Region:
92–4 Tooley Street,
London SE1 9SH.
Telephone (071) 403 4111

Southern Regional Office:
72a London Street,
Reading, RG1 4SD.
Telephone Reading (0734) 587345

7 Training packs

The Education Department of the British Epilepsy Association has produced a useful training pack for teachers entitled *Epilepsy: Children and young people with epilepsy.*

The pack contains a video, acetates for group instruction and a range of booklets, the titles of which include:

(a) Epilepsy: a guide for teachers

(b) What difference does it make, Danny? (provides a delightful story of Danny, a young child with epilepsy, and his adventures)

(c) Living with epilepsy

(d) The medical management of epilepsy

(e) Suggestions for lessons and stimulus material.

8 Useful reading

FAMILY FUND (1987) *After 16 – What next?* (York: Joseph Rowntree Memorial Trust).

HOPKINS, A. (1981) *Epilepsy: The Facts* (Oxford: OUP).

KETTLE, M. and MASSIE, B. (1986) *Employer's Guide to Disabilities* (London: Royal Association for Disability and Rehabitation – RADAR).

KURTZ, Z. and RICHMAN, N. (1989) 'Children with epilepsy who have special educational needs', *Children and Society*, 3, 2, 139 51.

LAIDLAW, J. and M. (1980) *Epilepsy Explained* (Edinburgh: Churchill–Livingstone).

MCGOVERN, S. (1981) *The Epilepsy Handbook* (London: Sheldon Press).

MALE, J. and THOMPSON, C. (1985) *The Educational Implications of Disability*, A guide for teachers (London: RADAR).

THE NATIONAL ADVISORY COUNCIL ON THE EMPLOYMENT OF DISABLED PEOPLE (1985) *The additional employment problems of young disabled people.*

SCOTT, D. (1981) *About Epilepsy*, 4th edn, (London: Duckworth).

THOMPSON, M. (1986) *Employment for Disabled People* (London: Kogan Page).

CASE STUDY 8

Sandra

A thirteen-year-old child with severe learning difficulties

The following work was carried out in the context of a workshop for the entire teaching staff of a school for children with severe learning difficulties. The workshop consisted of six after-school meetings on a weekly basis, with visits to the classroom by the organising psychologist between sessions. Aims and objectives, concepts and implementation were discussed, and each teacher chose a study child, attempted to apply the concepts with that child and reported back regularly. The psychologist discussed in detail with individual teachers programmes for, and progress of, their study children.

Mrs Bay taught in a 'special care' class, that is a class for children with severe handicaps both mentally and physically. She chose to work with a thirteen-year-old girl called Sandra, who had cerebral palsy. She had hardly any use of her legs and a very limited use of her arms. She could not sit up on her own or even roll over. Though she had no speech, she was alert and interested in the world, and Mrs Bay felt she had quite a lot of understanding and some ability to communicate by making sounds.

The first step was to identify and record some general aims which should guide Sandra's education. Mrs Bay selected the following:

- Improve relationships with more able children so that she could mix with them and receive more stimulation than was available in the special care class.
- Improve motor skills, particularly hand/arm skills.
- Help erase frustrations due to lack of communicative speech.
- Enable her to have a more independent life with free movement in a wheel-chair.

These general aims now had to be used as a basis for defining particular teaching needs. First, teachers were asked to identify general areas of functioning which needed to be developed to help move towards the aims. Mrs Bay thought that help was most needed in motor development, in development of communication and in development of social skills. All of these were important, but, to focus attention on the concepts the workshop was helping the teachers to learn and apply, it was suggested that one area should be selected for special study and recording. Mrs Bay chose motor development. When asked to focus on one main aspect of motor development, she chose arm and hand movements, and, in particular, those involved in operating a wheelchair.

The next step was to move from the general to the very specific by selecting teaching objectives, distinguished from aims by being clearly described tasks whose achievement could be demonstrated by careful observation of the child within a reasonable short time. The objectives were to be arranged in a progressive series, so that, having mastered one, the child could be regarded as ready to proceed to the next. Mrs Bay chose the following sequence:

- Touch wheel of wheelchair.
- Grasp wheel of wheelchair.
- Move wheel of wheelchair backwards (her physical disabilities suggested that moving it forwards would be too difficult initially).
- Move wheel of wheelchair forwards.

Careful testing and observation showed that she could already touch the wheel, but could not grasp or move it. Grasping the wheel was therefore the next objective to teach. Sometimes an objective needs dividing into component 'subtasks' before teaching, but this was not the case here. Grasping the wheel was, therefore, the actual task to be taught in a teaching session – and was therefore referred to as a 'teaching unit'.

The teaching unit now had to be subjected to a 'teaching analysis', which required identification of what the child needed to attend to, what actions were required of the child, what guiding strategies were needed from the teacher, and what reward strategies the teacher needed to use. For Sandra these were:

- *Attend to* – sitting position, hands, fingers, position of wheel in relation to arms.
- *Actions required* – moving to sitting position, moving arm.
- *Guiding strategies* – verbal instructions, demonstration of hand movements required.
- *Reward strategies* – praise, being 'made up' in front of a mirror.

She was, therefore, guided as often as possible each day to attend and act as indicated and systematically rewarded for successes by praise and 'being made up'. Within a few months, she was able to find and grasp the wheel with her left hand.

It was now possible to concentrate on moving the wheel. This task was analysed in much the same way, and, using the same kinds of guiding and reward strategies, she rapidly learned to turn the wheel backwards with her left hand – sufficiently to make the wheelchair go round in a circle. Unfortunately, she then spent a period in hospital and on her return, seemed physically incapable of doing what she had learned. With the help of the visiting physiotherapist, it was found that, if the wheelchair sides were removed and she was held in by straps, she could reach and grasp the wheel more easily. Progress was then resumed, with concentration on the right hand. At first, because of the particular nature of her spastic condition, it rotated in the wrong direction when moved towards the wheel, but, with continued advice and help from the physiotherapist, and much practice over a six-month period, she was eventually able to propel the wheelchair backwards using both hands. This was about eighteen months after the beginning of the project.

Mrs Bay subsequently applied the approach to Sandra's eating and communication – and also to the needs of other children in the class.

QUESTIONS

1 To what range of educational activities could objectives approaches usefully be applied?

2 How useful could these approaches be in mainstream schools?

3 Could similarly clear objectives be formulated for creative activities such as painting or such educational experiences as listening to music? If not, what other devices might be used to ensure that such educational experiences are relevant to a child's needs?

4 Is it better to teach physically handicapped children to use artificial means of moving about, or should they be taught instead to use more natural means, such as walking, however slowly and clumsily, or crawling?

SUPPORTIVE INFORMATION AND MATERIAL

1 A basic text on teaching through objectives is:

AINSCOW, M. and TWEDDLE, D. (1979) *Preventing Classroom Failure: An Objectives Approach* (Chichester: John Wiley).

2 The general principles on which the workshop above was based are outlined in:

PRESLAND, J. and ROBERTS, G. (1980) 'Aims, objectives and ESN (S) children', *Special Education: Forward Trends*, 7, 2, 29–31.

3 Other accounts can be found in:

COUPE, J. and PORTER, J. (1986) *The Education of Children with Severe Learning Difficulties* (London: Croom Helm).

GARDNER, J., MURPHY, J. and CRAWFORD, N. (1983) *The Skills Analysis Model: An Effective Curriculum for Children with Severe Learning Difficulties* (Kidderminster: BIMH Publications).

PERKINS, E., TAYLOR, P. and CAPIE, A. (1980) *Helping the Retarded: A Systematic Behavioural Approach*, 2nd edition (Kidderminster: BIMH Publications).

PRESLAND, J.L. (1989) *Paths to Mobility in 'Special Care': A Guide to Teaching Gross Motor Skills to Very Handicapped Children*, 2nd edition (Kidderminster: BIMH Publications).

RAYMOND, J. (1984) *Teaching the Child with Special Needs* (London: Ward Lock).

4   Other examples of work from the workshop and a similar enterprise are described in:

PRESLAND, J. (1979) 'Aims and Objectives into practice with Severe Learning Difficulties' in Stratford, R. (ed.) *Recent developments in Special Education, Proceedings of DECP Annual Course*, British Psychological Society Division of Educational and Child Psychology, pp. 40–44.

PRESLAND, J. and FARREN, A. (1983) 'Working with Jasper: applying the concepts of an aims and objectives workshop', *Mental Handicap*, 12, 1, 32–4.

PRESLAND, J. (1982) 'Applying psychology to teaching the 3Rs: opening address at DECP course at York University, January 1982', *Occasional Papers of the British Psychological Society Division of Educational and Child Psychology*, 6, 1, 3–13.

PRESLAND, J. (1989) 'Advising on children with profound and multiple handicaps', *Educational Psychology in Practice*, in press.

5   Checklists to help in selecting teaching objectives with this population include:

BLUMA, S., SHEARER, J., FROHMAN, A. and HILLIARD, J. (1976) *Portage Guide to Early Education*. (Windsor: NFER-Nelson).

GUNSTONE, C. (1985) *The Anson House Pre-School Project: The Revised Checklist* (London: Barnardo's).

JEFFREE, D. and CHESELDINE, S. (1982) *Paths to Independence: Checklists of Self-help and Social Skills* (London: Hodder and Stoughton).

JEFFREE, D.M. and McCONKEY, R. (1976) *PIP Developmental Charts* (London: Hodder and Stoughton).

JENKINS, J., FELCE, D., MANSELL, J., FLIGHT, L. and DELL, D. (1983) *The Bereweeke Skill-teaching System* (Windsor: NFER-Nelson).

PERKINS, E.A., TAYLOR, P.D. and CAPIE, A.C.M. (1980) *Developmental Checklist*, 2nd edition (Kidderminster: BIMH Publications).

PRESLAND, J. (1989) *The Paths to Mobility Checklist: Objectives for Teaching Gross Motor Skills to 'Special Care' Children*, 2nd edition (Kidderminster: BIMH Publications).

SIMON, G.B. (1981) *The Next Step on the Ladder*, 3rd edition (Kidderminster: BIMH Publications).

WARNER, J. (1981) *Feeding Checklist* (Buckingham: Winslow Press).

WHITE, M. and EAST, K. (1983) *The Wessex Revised Portage Language Checklist* (Windsor: NFER–Nelson).

6 Other work on planning and implementing educational programmes for pupils with severe learning difficulties is described by:

GILLHAM, B. (1987) *A Basic Attainments Programme for Young Mentally Handicapped Children* (London: Croom Helm).

THATCHER, J. (1984) *Teaching Mentally Handicapped Children to Read* (London: Cassell).

UPTON, G. (1979) *Physical and Creative Activities for the Mentally Handicapped* (Cambridge: Cambridge University Press).

CASE STUDY 9

Twinely District

A Primary Heads' In-Service Training day

1 Twenty-four Primary Headteachers of the district assembled for a one-day conference organised by the local education authority, and led by a county adviser. The hall of a large Primary School was the setting, and the majority of the Heads of the district were present, most of them knowing each other well. Some six or seven of the Heads were fairly recent appointments. Church Aided Schools Heads were present, with a number of state infant and junior schools.

The following programme timings were followed:

9.15–9.30	assemble and introduction
9.30–10.30	Session One
10.30–10.45	Break for coffee
10.45–12.15	Session Two
12.15–1.00	Lunch break in school
1.00–2.00	Session Three
2.00–2.15	Break
2.45–3.45	Session Four
3.45–4.00	Tea and disperse

2 The title of the course was 'Learning and Pupil Development', and the aim was to challenge the approaches of schools which were largely traditional in style. A similar day for Primary School Deputy Heads, each accompanied by one of their staff, was arranged a month after the Headteachers' conference.

3 The setting was kept fairly mobile, with a changing pattern of groups, and the work done was in the form of short talks, based on a handout given to all participants. There were frequent breaks for discussions and questions.

4 The basic human needs were discussed first, and adult and children's needs compared. The following were considered:

- Health
- Security
- Privacy
- Affection
- Being valued
- Learning
- Qualifications
- Skills

The school's primary function of learning and its parallel function of caring for the pupil's personal development were emphasised. The fundamental link between successful learning and good personal relationships and satisfactory child development continued to be emphasised throughout the day.

5   Some definitions were briefly discussed: health education, social education, family life education, education in personal relationships, personal and social education. The balance of the primary curriculum was discussed, as were tests of attainment. Adult recollections of our own childhood development were questioned, and the following concepts reviewed:

- Temperament
- Personality
- Reference groups
- Models of behaviour
- Effect of environment
- The family blueprint.

6   What do children need from a school? Steadfast values and practices or challenging ones? How can a school deal with the differing needs of children from widely differing backgrounds, to ensure that learning takes place. Is change, in fact, needed? The conference was reminded of the challenges to family and school in our rapidly changing society:

- Materialism
- Secularism
- Egalitarianism
- New technology
- Media power
- Multi-cultural society
- Changing sex roles
- Changing family life
- Challenges to authority

7   Suggested views on the future of society were discussed, using Hopson and Scally's Life Skills Teaching (McGraw Hill, 1981).

- Providing and receiving knowledge and skills – the major growth area
- Unemployment
- Discretionary time increased
- Overchoice and 'future shock'
- Increased interdependence and effective communication skills essential
- Personal relationships more temporary
- A new concept of work
- New concept of career
- Changed concept of 'welfare state'
- Adaptable labour force – to exercise initiative and generate commitment
     (i)   3 – 4 occupations
     (ii)   9 – 10 job changes
     (iii) Moves away from home area
     (iv)   Two marriages
     (v)   Continuing education
     (vi)   Unemployment at some time
     (vii) Changing job patterns
- *Greater range of personal competencies essential.*

8   As well as learning skills, can a primary school develop *living* skills, to meet some of these challenges in the future life of the children?

- Language to say what we mean and feel
- Knowledge about behaviour
- Social competence skills
- Learning to live with one's personality
- Learning to be an individual and a group member
- Decision-making skills.

The varying influences of family, school and environment were again discussed.

9   What living skills could be taught in a Primary School to enable pupils to comprehend and deal with such topics as:

- Aggression
- Deviance and abnormalities in human behaviour
- Mental illness
- Sex education and sexuality
- Drug and alcohol misuse
- Prejudice
- Bereavement
- Happiness!

and with concerns such as:
- Smoking
- Home safety
- Personal development
- First aid in accidents
- Hygiene
- Helping the handicapped
- Cancer knowledge
- Diet.

The wide variety of topics in such living skills was considered, and the impossibility of dealing with everything emphasised. How then does a school decide which topics are possible and necessary?

10   How can such work in schools be done?

- Implicit in the normal curriculum
- Time-tabled curriculum periods
- Occasional courses
- By all staff? Selected staff? Visiting experts?
- By team work and co-ordination?

11   Further examples of varying school approaches were discussed, particularly in health education syllabuses. Heads contributed their own approaches, and

the local authority's policy in various matters was discussed. The responsibilities of the Headteacher and Governors were discussed.

12   What problems arise?
What is 'normal'?
What is an invasion of privacy?
What is solely a family's business?
What is the link with learning?
What precisely is the school's role?
What evaluation and assessment is possible in these areas?

13   The following issues were explored:

The attitudes of teachers in a school
Preparation of staff
Use of other agencies
Visual aids and books
Parents' involvement

14   Sex education was discussed, using the following points as the basis for discussion:

Sex education attracts attention, perhaps unwarranted.
- Earlier maturity and sophistication of junior children
- Pressures on children from society
- Parental responsibility paramount – *every* home teaches about sexuality
- Majority of parents find interpretation and teaching about sex difficult?
- Most children learn from other children?
- Erroneous ideas and selfish, exploitive attitudes reduce and cheapen sex, and are difficult to correct later
- Schools to do something positive, to help parents in a complementary way? Intrusive?
- *Plowden*: 'It is not good enough to leave matters vague and open, hoping for the best'.
- Must be in setting of family life and caring relationships – teachers' attitude and personality is a major factor.

15   The Primary School's work leads to a preparation for the Secondary School world, and adolescence.

Adolescence
- *Realising physical maturity* – Puberty
   Clumsiness
   Earlier Maturity
- Establishing an acceptable *sex role*, understanding opposite sex
- Developing social skills – *social competence*
   Contemporaries – subcultures – gangs

- Developing *emotional maturity* and independence
- Achieving *intellectual maturity* – potential.
  Achievement
- Gaining *emancipation from home control* – economic independence – self-control
- Selecting *occupation* –abilities, strengths, opportunities
- Using *leisure*
- Discovering a *philosophy of life*
- Discovering *self-identity – self-esteem*.

16   In conclusion the following points were raised:

The social power of the teacher and the potential influence of schools.
The effect of the quality of leadership, and the quality of the teachers.
The hidden curriculum, and the informal curriculum.
The effect of the ethos of the school, and of the total curriculum.

Are schools cynics or guardians of skills for living?
- Knowledge of life skills can be provided
- Attitudes can be discussed and developed
- Habits can be encouraged
- Values can be suggested
- Teachers provide models whether they like it or not
- The school can remain as a reference group in the child's memory.

Maturity can be an aim. A school matter? Home and family matter?
The capacity to:
- enjoy relationships
- live and work without too much inner tension
- tolerate anxiety
- tolerate opposition or criticism
- live without causing too much tension in others
- to see events and people as they really are
- to tolerate differing moral environments.

QUESTIONS

1   What reactions might be expected from Headteachers?

2   What questions are they likely to ask?

3   Is there too much material for the time available?

4   What can make such an In-Service Training day successful?

5   What is missing from the day?

6   What effect will the national curriculum and assessment procedures have on such personal and social development?

SUPPORTIVE INFORMATION AND MATERIAL

1   A selection of normal themes in personal and social education

(a)   *Personal*

Personal Hygiene	Nutrition and Diet
Fitness, Exercise and Rest	Standards of personal behaviour
Personal Appearance	Growth and Development
Dental Health	Understanding ourselves
Internal working of the Body	Decision-making
Care of feet, ears, hair	Personal values and attitudes

(b)   *Community*

Cancer education	Handicapped people
Diseases	First Aid
Obesity	The Elderly
Sexually transmitted diseases	Mental Health and Stress
Alcohol and Alcoholism	World Health
Drug taking	Food Hygiene
Smoking	Noise
Health Services and Public Health	Multi-cultural aspects of Health
Medicines and common illnesses	

(c)   *Environment*

Road Safety	Pollution
Safety in the Home	Law and Order
Safety at Work	Mass Media and its effect
Water Safety	Consumer education
Conservation	

(d)   *Family life and personal relationship*

Feelings and needs of other people	Care of young children
Tolerance	Sexual relationships
Friendship	Birth control and abortion
Anxiety and Stress	Work and leisure
Preparation for marriage and Parenthood	Reproduction and birth
	Home-making
Family life	

2   A random list of topics which might arise at various times in personal and social education

Such a list can be used with teachers' groups:

(a) to view individually, assessing one's personal reactions

(b) to discuss with others:
- what topics are inappropriate in Primary Schools? Secondary Schools?
- what topics require 'experts'?
- which themes embarrass adults? Children?
- which arise in normal teaching?

Hygiene	Alcohol	Personal relationships
Use of the Doctor	Anatomy of the human	Stealing
Unemployment	body	Lying
Human development	Birth	Cancer education
Love	Safety with chemicals in	Leisure
Marriage	the home	Aids
Money	Communication	Nutrition
The media	Conception	Conservation
Management of the	Contraception	Smoking
home	Drugs and medicines	Pollution
Homosexuality	Imprisonment	Dental Health
Race	Health Services	Abortion
Mental health	Death	Belief in God
Relationships	Diseases	Unions
Responsibility	Emotions	Healing
Sexuality	Exercise	Understanding society
Vandalism	Slimming	Different jobs
Road Safety	First Aid	Poverty
Home Safety	Patterns of family life	Law
Play Safety	Influence of groups	Life in cities
Play	Handicapped people	

3   A checklist of themes for courses in upper classes of Primary Schools, in Middle Schools and in Secondary Schools   P|

(a) Possible titles of courses

Education in Personal Relationships	Personal Guidance
Family Life Education	Health Education
Social and Personal Education	General Studies
Moral and Social Education	

(b) Selected material can be the basis of:

- a regular timetabled series
- regular tutorial work, co-ordinated with subject teaching
- short courses at appropriate times
- co-ordinated work throughout several teaching departments, each accepting

responsibility for certain topics or sections of topics at certain times
- occasional residential experience courses
- informal discussions in clubs or leisure settings.

(c) Techniques include:

- Gaining rapport with the group
- Spending some time on teaching but more on purposeful discussion
- Being prepared for questions of an unexpected nature
- Being conversant with the attitudes of the young and having some understanding of the language they use
- The teacher expressing personal convictions, positively and sincerely, when they are sought and when they are appropriate.

(d) The general aim:

To help pupils to find information about human behaviour, to examine the values which people have found lead to personal happiness and stability in our society, and to encourage them to develop standards of personal morality.

(e) The objectives of the teacher:

- To inform the pupils about themselves and their growing powers of mind and body.
- To help them form and develop stable relationships with others, accept other people and appreciate the value of tolerance.
- To help them face relationships with authority, with other adults and with the other sex.
- To widen their horizons to the problems of humanity and to awaken an awareness of their responsibility towards neighbours and community.
- To encourage pupils to explore and appreciate other people's beliefs, while developing their own.
- To create a climate of opinion that these themes are vitally important.
- Occasionally to act as counsellors for individuals, recognising those who require special help.

1   PERSONAL DEVELOPMENT

(a)   The body and how it works – human biology.

(b)   Reproduction and birth in the setting of family life and caring relationships.

(c)   The growth and development of babies and children.

(d)   Physical growth to maturity.

(e)   Puberty – physical and psychological changes in adolescence.

(f)   Emotional development.

2 THE INDIVIDUAL

(a)   Special advantages Man has over other animals.

(b)   Learning processes and memory.

(c)   Development of individual personalities.

(d)   Moods and emotions.

(e)   The influence of heredity and environment.

(f)   Will-power and understanding ourselves.

(g)   Self-control and co-operation are essential for a civilised life.

(h)   Conscience and personal standards of responsibility.

(i)   How important is it to be an individual?

3 PERSONAL BEHAVIOUR

(a)   Standards of personal behaviour with reference to the following:

(b)   Exploitation of others;

(c)   Bullying;

(d)   Disobedience and rebellion against authority;

(e)   Jealousy and vindictiveness;

(f)   Shyness;

(g)   Facing adversity;

(h)   Fear and submissiveness;

(i)   Desire for security;

(j)   Conceit and possessiveness;

(k)   Greed;

(l)   Respect for others in family and circle of friends;

(m)   Codes of behaviour;

(n)   Are there changing standards and values?

(o)   Why do people behave badly – insecurity, ignorance, fear, nervousness?

(p)   Good manners and courtesy;

(q)   Social responsibility in a community.

4 PERSONAL AND COMMUNITY HEALTH

(a)   Personal fitness and exercise – leisure pursuits – rest – posture.

(b)   Personal discipline and responsibility.

(c)   Personal hygiene and health habits – cleanliness and personal attraction.

(d)   Food and diet – over and under-weight – cholesterol levels. Food hygicnc.

(e)   Suitable clothing – fashion.

(f)   Foot care and shoes.

(g)   Dental health and fluoridation.

(h)   Care of skin and hair.

(i)   Care of eyes – colour blindness.

(j)   Hearing – infections – impairments – aids – noise.

(k)   Dirt and danger in smoking.

(l)   Common illnesses and home nursing. Major diseases and community health – invalids, immunisation.

(m)   Sexually transmitted diseases.

(n)   Handicaps: mental and physical, attitudes, causes, effects, treatment, rehabilitation.

(o)   Cancer education.

(p)   Alcohol and drugs education.

(q)   Road safety.

(r)   Home safety: common accidents and their prevention.

(s)   Safety in outdoor pursuits, including personal survival.

(t)   Elementary First Aid.

(u)   Safety at work. Shops and Factory Acts.

(v)   Parenthood.

5 PERSONAL RELATIONSHIPS

(a)   Need for affection, recognition and acceptance.

(b)   Self-understanding – knowing one's faults and limitations – developing personal potential and ways of coping with life.

(c)   Need to live and co-operate with others. The words we use.

(d)   How do we behave towards people we dislike and like?

(e)   Loneliness in ourselves and others.

(f)   Making friends – need to give as well as seek friendship.

(g)   Recognising roles and attitudes, and the need to present oneself well to others.

(h)   Boy–girl relationships. Sexual attraction, socially acceptable behaviour, courtship, recognition of courtesy and respect, exploitation and selfishness.

6 FRIENDSHIP

(a)   What is a friend? What is an acquaintance?

(b)   Discuss the meaning of true friendship – giving as well as taking.

(c)   Self-understanding.

(d)   What qualities do you expect in a friend?

(e)   What qualities do you have which make you a good friend?

(f)   Discuss changes in friendship of group members within the last five years. Why do these changes take place?

(g)   Can we be attracted by someone we do not like? By someone we do not know?

(h)   Discuss the differences of reaction to overtures of friendship between men and women.

(i)   Friendships in groups, gangs and clubs. Pressures to conform. Status and role within groups.

(j)   Friendships with the opposite sex. Status symbol of dating; steady or casual relationships. Friendship as part of marriage.

7 RELATIONSHIPS WITH OTHERS

(a)   What is a group? Types of groups. The family group. The structure and functions of groups in the local community. The gregarious nature and interdependence of man. 'In' groups and 'out' groups. School groups.

(b)   Unorganised groups. Mass thinking and mob law. Irrational behaviour in a crowd. Gang bravado and panic in crowds. Formation of public opinion.

(c)   Deviant groups. Homosexuals. Gypsies. Minorities. 'Not our sort' – our reactions. Sterotyping.

(d)   The handicapped and their needs.

(e)   Class, racial and religious prejudices in relationships.

8 SEXUAL RELATIONSHIPS

(a)   Sex education and human biology.

(b)   Sexuality, attitudes and values. Sex kept in perspective.

(c)   Sex roles.

(d)   Chastity and promiscuity.

(f)   Loving someone and being in love with someone.

(g)   Premarital intercourse.

(h)   Pregnancy outside marriage.

(i)   Homosexuality.

(j)   Contraception and abortion.

(k)   Sexually transmitted diseases.

(l)   Sexual behaviour and courtesy; mutual respect; exploitation and selfishness.

(m)   The effect of alcohol, group pressures and drugs on behaviour.

9 FAMILY LIFE

(a)   Growing up in the family – the importance of play for pre-school children. The family socialises children. The family as a sheltered environment.

(b)   Foster children, adopted children, only children, unwanted children.

(c)   How do members of a family behave towards each other?

(d)   What is family loyalty?

(e)   Discuss family loyalty in large and small families.

(f)   Make a list of causes of family friction.

(g)   Bringing friends home.

(h)   Parties.

(i)   Parents' rules – understanding parents.

(j)   The family as a social institution. Family trees.

(k)   Comparison of British family today with that of other cultures.

(l)   Extended and nuclear families.

(m) Factors affecting marriage and the family partnerships, birth rate, family size.

(n) Age at marriage.

(o) Women at work.

(p) Differences between social classes, religious denominations and countries.

(q) Problem families.

(r) Communes.

(s) The elderly.

(t) How are the traditional roles of men and women changing?

(u) School and home co-operation.

(v) Parentcraft.

(w) Home-making.

10 MARRIAGE

(a) Engagements. Liking same things (perhaps in a different way), looking at things in the same way; behaviour in the same things (morals, religion). People of different religions, morals, interests. Length of time to find out compatibility.

(b) Anticipating the problems of marriage. Living with one person for many years. Tolerance, sympathy, love, kindness, companionship. What other qualities would you expect of a partner?

(c) Teenage, mixed and arranged marriages. Ideals of love. Adolescent and adult viewpoints.

(d) Commitment and companionship.

(e) Rights and duties of wife and husband. Changing roles of men and women. Mothers at work.

(f) Home-making. Mortgages and hire purchase. Family and personal budgeting. Pocket-money.

(g) Divorce and separation. Living alone by choice.

(h) Parenthood. Adoption. Family planning.

11 INTOLERANCE

(a) Prejudice – how is it formed? Family background? Mass media? Steretyping?

(b) Sense of security of belonging to a group. Do we reject what is outside our group. 'Not our sort'. Often any person found doing wrong is associated with a group – is this fair? Class discrimination.

(c)   Racial problems.

(d)   Inter-racial marriages.

(e)   Amicable relationships at school, work or leisure, with people having different views on politics and religion.

(f)   Jealousy, hatred, conceit, bullying.

12   LEISURE

(a)   What is leisure?

(b)   The shorter working week.

(c)   Constructive and destructive uses of leisure.

(d)   Social obligations.

(e)   Rest and relaxation.

(f)   Boredom.

(g)   Laziness.

(h)   'My time's my own'.

(i)   Local leisure facilities for the various age groups.

(j)   Changes in leisure activities.

(k)   Leisure patterns in different social classes and in different occupations.

(l)   Individual and shared leisure activities.

(m)   Wasting time – has inactivity a positive value?

(n)   How does use of leisure make work for others?

(o)   Misuse – pornography, gambling, drunkenness.

(p)   Voluntary work can:
- Counteract tendency to passive acceptance of 'laid on' systems of service and entertainments;
- Give opportunity to co-operate and mix with others – mutual understanding.
- Humanise public affairs;
- Give experience in responsibility and administration.

(q)   Future happiness compared with present satisfaction.

13 WORK

(a) The value of further education and training. The problem of friends who ignore this and in the early years earn more money. Ambition.

(b) Careers for girls and married women. Equal rights legislation.

(c) Interviews. Careers guidance. Self-assessment.

(d) Problems of leaving home. Problems of living at home.

(e) Health and accommodation problems. Loneliness.

(f) Working conditions of today and yesterday. Technological change and its consequences for the individual and society. Legislation protecting people at work. Rights and obligations at work.

(g) Getting on with people at work. Understanding work discipline.

(h) Trade unions and their relationships with individuals and with society. Industrial relationships.

(i) Employers and their expectations and needs. Relationships with foreman and management.

(j) Rewards of standards of work – job satisfaction. Training.

(k) 'Only mugs work hard.' Is work a good thing in itself? Economic incentives alone produce neither willing workers nor good craftsmanship.

(l) Unemployment: social services schemes.

(m) The need for personal convictions and standards of one's own.

14 AUTHORITY

(a) Imagine yourself in a position of authority. What difficulties might you encounter if you were;
- a headwaiter
- a foreman
- an employer
- a police sergeant.

(b) What is the basis of authority?
- Within school or workplace;
- Within home;
- Within the community.

(c) Self-control, will-power, and conscience are bases of authority?

(d) Why do authorities impose standards of behaviour?

(e)   Young people and the Law. Age and legal status.

(f)   Petty and organised crime. Delinquency. Vandalism. The courts and probation. Violence – cause and effect. Prevention or punishment? The police – duties, powers, obligations. Cost of crime to the community.

(g)   Registering a legal protest against authority. Newspapers. Ombudsmen. Pressure Groups. Duties and Rights. Race Relations Acts. Trade Descriptions Act. The Sale of Goods Act. Weights and Measures Act. Food and Drugs Act. Hire Purchase Regulations. The Consumer Council. Citizens Advice Bureaux. Other consumer societies and groups.

15   FREEDOM

(a)   How important is freedom? How is it related to responsibilities?

(b)   Can there be real freedom without the existence of risks – accidents, disease, unhappiness?

(c)   Choosing a career – what do we look for – security, prospects, money, service?

(d)   When you start earning money, how does your home situation change?

(e)   What prevents you being treated as an adult?

(f)   Should you always be treated as an adult, and how much responsibility for this falls on you. The reasons for rules.

(g)   Does 'becoming an adult' depend only on size and age?

(h)   Discuss respect for other people and their ideas. Balance between 'my' freedom and 'their' freedom.

(i)   Behaviour with older people, parents, opposite sex, one's own friends, colleagues.

(j)   Changing standards and values. Does absence of manners denote immaturity?

(k)   Why do people behave badly – insecurity, ignorance, fear, nervousness?

(l)   Is freedom a privilege or a right?

16   ENVIRONMENT CONTROL AND COMMUNITY CARE

(a)   Pollution of the environment; its causes, effects and methods of control – air, water, food and living conditions.

(b)   National Health Service and local health and welfare services.

(c)   School Health Service. Links with local health and welfare services.

(d)   Social services, both voluntary and statutory; voluntary organisations, voluntary social service work by young people.

(e)   World health and welfare; WHO, FAO, UNESCO, UNICEF, Red Cross, Oxfam, and other international organisations that deal with poverty and lack of education in developing countries. UN Charter.

(f)   Awareness and development of critical faculties. Creating a good environment. The development of critical awareness. Exploitation and manipulation by the mass media. Influence of film, radio, TV advertising, press and literature. Straight and crooked thinking.

(g)   Recent developments in education.

(h)   The Affluent Society. What is affluence? The development and problems of affluence. Possessions or people? Poverty in an affluent society. Gambling. Charity.

17   SOCIAL ENVIRONMENT

(a)   Population: fertility, adoption, abortion, birth control, morality, disease, diet, medicine.

(b)   Responsibilities to society: cultivating responsible attitudes.

(c)   Conservation of the environment: the individual's contribution as well as the efforts of authority and industry. Conflicting needs and demands.

(d)   Disease: history, infectious and non-infectious, control, common vectors of infection. Health hazards both in kinds of disease and precautions against them.

(e)   Chemical substances used in medicine: purpose of drugs in medication, dangers of self-medication, misuse and abuse of drugs and the dangers arising.

(f)   Addictive practices: alcohol, tobacco, cannabis, and the known addictive drugs. Gambling, physical and social effects. Social attitudes.

(g)   What is a good neighbour? Samaritans, Relate (Marriage Guidance), Alcoholics Anonymous, NSPCC, RSPCA.

18   THE ENVIRONMENT AFFECTS EVERYONE

Man as a technologist and as a farmer. World demands for energy. General development of machines and transport. Individuals and the State. Conservation movements. Urban problems. Effects of pollution. The future evolution of humans. World problems: population, hunger, poverty, disease, housing, apathy. Immigration and emigration. Ideologies and religions. Nationalism and internationalism. The need for 'communities'.

19 MORALITY AND HUMAN BEHAVIOUR

(a)   Living in a society of 'plural' values.

(b)   Why is there uncertainty?
       Overthrow of traditional value systems based on authority;
       religious authority; authority of moral codes.

(c)   What does it mean to be human?
       What are we for?
       Religious and non-religious views.

(d)   How do we decide what behaviour is right?
       The importance of rationality.

(e)   Can we agree on any marks of a morally educated man?
       for example, respect for other people translated into action (service).

(f)   Qualities men and women admire in others:
       - Love (Philia, Eros, Agape)
       - Patience
       - Faithfulness
       - Sacrifice
       - Courage
       - Faith
       Qualities men and women do not admire in others:
       - Hatred
       - Prejudice
       - Greed
       - Revenge
       - Sloth
       - Cowardice

(g)   Who should make the rules? Church, State?

(h)   What do I hope to achieve?

(i)   What does personal happiness mean?

(j)   What moral codes do we follow?

(k)   Is every human being vulnerable?

(l)   Does every human being have problems?

(m)   Need for recognition and acceptance by all.

4 Useful reading

BALDWIN, J. and WELLS, H. (1979–83) *Active Tutorial Work* (Oxford: Blackwell).

DAVID, K. and COWLEY, J. (1980) *Pastoral Care in Schools and Colleges* (Leeds: Edward Arnold).

DAVID, K. and CHARLTON, T. (1988) *The Caring Role of the Primary School* (Basingstoke: Macmillan).

DAVID, K. and WILLIAMS, T. (1987) *Health Education in Schools* (London: Harper and Row).

SCHOOLS COUNCIL (SCHEP) (1977) *Health Education Project 9–13 – Think Well* (Sunbury-on-Thames: Nelson).

CASE STUDY 10

Daniel

*A handicapped child in a
mainstream Secondary School*

Our son Daniel was born with Cerebral Palsy (CP), a condition resulting from damage to the brain just before, at, or just after birth. There are various types of CP depending upon which part of the brain was starved of oxygen. In Daniel's case he was left with athetosis, which means he has a great deal of uncontrolled movement. He cannot walk, use his hands or talk. Yet despite these crushing disabilities, he attends the local comprehensive school and is now studying for his GCSE examinations in eight subjects. Dependant upon his GCSE grades he enters the sixth form in September, 1989.

He has always preferred the company of the able bodied and he joined in all the activities of the local Cub Scout pack. Most of his friends are not disabled and he has a wide social circle.

Coupled to his gregarious nature are fine study skills and an enormous determination. The only control he has is the ability to use his feet accurately which allows him to press switches. At the age of three he was given a 'Possum' electric typewriter coupled to a scanning device which was controlled by foot switches. Learning took place quickly at his special school and his teachers reported a child with a quick mind. With the help of friends I converted what he was doing with the Possum machine onto an early microcomputer (the Acorn Atom). He then had simple editing facilities.The programme was developed, adding new ideas and converting it to the BBC 'B' machine when it became available. His primary education was at a small all-age special school for disabled children on a day basis. The teachers provided material that would stretch him academically, but were well aware that they probably could not provide the specialised teaching skills that he would need when eleven years old. He would have had a limited access to the curriculum. As teachers ourselves, we appreciated that changes had to be made at this age.

Following the 'Warnock Report' of 1978 came the 1981 Education Act. We had never considered that it would be possible to integrate Daniel into the mainstream of education, but with help from his special school Headteacher, and opposition from the Local Education Authority, he joined his present school at the age of eleven.

The comprehensive school displayed a deep sense of caring in its planning. Teachers were given INSET training into various disabilities and suggestions were made about how they could adapt their teaching styles to accommodate the disabled. It is to their credit that Daniel enjoyed his secondary schooling from the first day. It was a model of integration and we, his parents, owe a great deal of gratitude to the teachers and care staff. The authority provided an Acorn Master 128k computer and peripherals, a full-time assistant, and a part-time teacher. I provided a second set of foot switches and a copy of his computer programme. This meant that school work was done in school and homework at home. He was given an adapted curriculum in that he could not attend lessons like Art, CDT, Games and PE. It was during these lessons that Daniel could catch up with notes. Do not think that it has been problem free. Access to the upper part of the school provided some headaches until the authority provided him with a 'crawler'. This machine carries the wheelchair upstairs on two caterpillar wheels. Swimming sessions were arranged with a local school and this is Daniel's only activity lesson during the week.

The saddening part of the integration was the loss of speech therapy and physiotherapy. One can produce annual reviews year after year but if the service is provided by the Health Authority rather than the Education Authority, you can do little about such losses. This lack of service has resulted in a deterioration in Daniel's physical condition. It may be noted that some authorities have overcome this problem by employing their own therapists. We were well aware of the dangers involved in integration and had to make a choice.

Many feel that Daniel is employable. Only the future will tell. His computer system has continued to be improved, page turners fitted and shortly he is to be the proud user of an environmental control at home. This will allow him to control the whole house via the mains plugs, use the telephone, answer the door and unlock it should he wish. We are looking into a more portable computer system which will allow him to take notes within the classroom, and to fit a keyboard emulator to his computer (both made by Elphin Controls). Also there has to be more help with his communication. He uses a combination of 'Bliss Symbols' and his own spelling device. The new aid will have to be portable, easy to use, clearly understood and adaptable, Daniel is writing the software now as part of his course work for his GCSE but this only uses phonemes. There is a large payoff between cost and clarity in these aids. Most good ones (like the Touch Talker) are rather expensive. In the meanwhile Daniel's future development is being controlled more and more by Daniel himself.

Help has always been just around the corner. Parents are people too and recently my own Headmaster and his wife moved into our home to look after our two boys while we spent three glorious days in a luxury hotel. This was the first break we have had since our elder son was born sixteen years ago. Parents must always realise that society is keen to help and become involved. It is vital to the continuing level of care that parents are allowed to spend time away, time to themselves, to recharge batteries that are very heavily overloaded.

QUESTIONS

1   If you were due to receive an eleven-year-old child like Daniel into your school, how would you prepare your teaching staff? Among things to consider would be teaching styles, equipment, electrical points and access to buildings and rooms.

2   In a similar vein, it would be important to prepare the children. How would you approach this?

3   The 1981 Education Act speaks of provision for integration being 'reasonable' in terms of financial input. What would you consider reasonable?

4   Do you consider that the integration route taken by these parents was the correct one, considering there are residential special schools providing a full curriculum and GCSE examinations?

5   Should there have been a loss of speech therapy and physiotherapy after Daniel's integration into a 'normal' school? How could the withdrawal of this support have been justified?

SUPPORTIVE INFORMATION AND MATERIAL

1   General information

(a)   What is Cerebral Palsy?

Cerebral Palsy (sometimes referred to as spasticity) is an umbrella name that makes reference to a group of disorders that share a physical defect due to some type of damage inflicted upon the young and developing brain. This damage can be caused before birth, during birth, or after birth. While not all causes of cerebral palsy are known, of those that are known some three-quarters are known to have been caused during pre- or peri-natal periods.

(b)   Some possible causes of cerebral palsy.

(i)   *Pre-natal*
Toxoplasmosis
Rubella (German measles)
Herpes simplex

(ii)   *Peri-natal*
asphyxia/hypoxia – lack of oxygen supply to brain

(iii)   *Post-natal*
Meningitis or encephalitis (infection of the brain)
Injuries to the brain

(c)   How common is cerebral palsy?

Reliable estimates suggest 2.4 : 10 000 births

(d)   What types of cerebral palsy are there?

(i)   hemiplegia – affects one side of the body ⎫
(ii)   diplegia – affects both legs   ⎬ spastic cerebral palsy
(iii) quadriplegia – affects all four limbs   ⎭
(iv)   athetosis – slow, sometimes, writhing movements in small muscles such as hands
(v)   chorea – more rapid, jerky movements, more marked in large muscles such as shoulders
(vi)   dystonia – sudden stiffening movements and postures which may affect the whole body.

2   These are contacts parents have found useful.

These would have to be contacted in your local area.

- Social Worker
- Occupational Therapist (gaining access to equipment, chairs, etc.)
- Medical professionals: GP, paediatrician, speech therapist, physiotherapist
- Educational professionals: Headteacher, classteacher, adviser for Special Educational Needs, educational psychologist
- Local branch of the Spastics association
- Other specialised societies according to the child's problem.

3   Useful addresses

(a)   Excellent electronic controls
Elphin Controls,
Llantony Road Trading Estate,
Gloucester.
Telephone Gloucester 411533

(c)   Touch Communication Aid
Blissymbolics Communication
  Resource Centre (UK)
South Glamorgan Institute of
  Higher Education,
Western Avenue,
Llandaff,
Cardiff, CF5 2YB.

(b)   Touch Talker
Liberator Ltd.
Whitegates,
Swinstead,
Lincs. NG33 4PA

OR

The Blissymbol Programme,
Heathfield School,
Oldbury Way,
Fareham,
Hants. PO14 3BN.

(d) *Chairs and other aids, fitted specifically for the user*
Mary Marlborough Lodge,
Nuffield Orthopaedic Centre,
Headington,
Oxford, OX3 7LD

(e) *Further Education*
The National Star Centre College of Further Education,
Ullenwood Manor,
Cheltenham,
Gloucester, GL53 9QU
Telephone Cheltenham (0242) 527631

(f) *National Body overseeing Educational Software*
MESU (Microelectronics Educational Support Unit),
Unit 6,
Sir William Lyons Road,
Science Park,
University of Warwick,
Coventry, CV4 7EZ.
Telephone Coventry (0203) 416994

(g) *Computer programs and switching aids specific to the child*
The Ace Centre,
Ormerod School,
Waynflete Road,
Headington,
Oxford, OX3 8DD.
Telephone Oxford (0865) 63508

(h) *Provider of aids supplied by the DHSS*
Possum Controls,
63 Mandeville Road,
Aylesbury,
Bucks, HP21 8AE.
Telephone Aylesbury (0296) 81591

(i) *Help with aids from Possum, not provided by the DHSS*
The Possum Trust,
Administrator,
14 Greenvale Drive,
Timsbury,
Bath, BA3 1HP.
Telephone Bath (0761) 71184

(j) *Charity to help provide aids for the disabled*
SEQUAL,
Administrator,
Block 178,
Milton Trading Estate,
Abingdon,
Oxon. OX14 4ES.
Telephone (0235) 833193

(k) *Manufacturer of computers*
Acorn Computers Ltd.,
Fulbourn Road,
Cherry Hinton,
Cambridge, CB1 4JN.

(l)   *Help with communication problems*
Assistive Communication
  Aids Centre,
Frenchay Hospital,
Bristol.

RADAR (Royal Association for Disability and Rehabilitation)
25 Mortimer Street,
London, W1N 8AB.

SEMERC (Special Education Micro-Electronics Resource Centre)
Faculty of Education,
Bristol Polytechnic,
Redland Hill,
Bristol, BS6 6U2.
(There are other SEMERCs in other parts of the country).

REMAP (Rehabilitation Engineering Movement Advisory Panel)
Thames House North,
London, SW1P 4QG.

Disabled Living Foundation,
346 Kensington High Street,
London, W14 8NS.

4   Other useful organisations

(a)   *British Sports Association for the Disabled (BSAD),*
Stoke Mandeville Stadium,
Harvey Road,
Aylesbury,
Bucks.

(b)   *Cheyne Holiday Club for Handicapped Children,*
61 Cheyne Walk,
Chelsea,
London, SW3 5LK.
Telephone 071 352 8434

(c)   *Voluntary Council for Handicapped Children,*
8 Wakley Street,
London, EC1V 7QB.
Telephone 071 278 9441

(d)   *Spastics Society,*
12 Park Crescent,
London, W1N 4EQ.
Telephone 071 636 5020

5   Useful references

(a)   The Warnock Report, (May 1978), HMSO,
49 High Holborn,
London, WC1V 6HB

(b)   The 1981 Education Act, HMSO,
49 High Holborn,
London, WC1V 6HB

CASE STUDY 11

Brian

A computer can help with the speech problems of a Secondary School child

Brian commenced his secondary education with a history of elective mutism. It was known that he was capable of speech because he spoke to his mother, and very occasionally to other children. It was considered to be possible that he could read, but what little written work he produced was indecipherable.

In a special needs class, he chose to sit alone, his face blank, unresponsive to questions either from the teacher or from other pupils. When asked to write about 'Myself', he wrote two lines in an hour and only occasional words were legible. It was most surprising to find, when he completed a Watts-Vernon Reading Test that Brian, aged 11.2 years, had a reading age of 14.8 years. When quietly praised for his good reading there was a flicker of response in his eyes and he nodded his head.

The first real breakthrough came when he was asked to write a story and told that he would be allowed to enter it into the computer and print it. He produced three lines of writing and was prepared to read them quietly to the teacher. This was the first time she had heard him speak and he was rewarded by being allowed to use the computer. He was shown how to use 'PEN DOWN' (Spear, 1986), but became frustrated because he could only type very slowly. When the teacher offered to type for him he accepted. He dictated, speaking slowly and very quietly. Soon he was trembling with excitement as the words of the story were quickly typed into the computer, displayed on the screen and then printed up in large jumbo print.

The computer was the motivating factor in much of Brian's slow but steady progress. Although he still chose to remain mute away from the computer, at the computer he was prepared to communicate with his peers in planning and writing group stories, or newspaper reports using 'FRONT PAGE EXTRA' (Keeling, 1985). He was prepared to lead his group and read to them when playing 'GRANNY'S GARDEN' (Matson, 1983), 'MALLORY' (Straker, 1985), or one of the many other programmes which are designed to improve reasoning, decision-making or literacy skills.

When the group used the computer to make a joke book it was discovered that Brian had an endless supply of jokes and he became the centre of attention in classroom and playground where he was persuaded to tell his jokes to an appreciative audience. When he was encouraged to tell his jokes to teachers and was rewarded by laughs of appreciation, he began to communicate with them a little more as well.

At the end of his first year in the Secondary School, Brian was prepared to answer direct questions. His handwriting was still laborious but to win the opportunity of using the computer he produced over a page of legible writing in an hour. When he became anxious he still had periods of withdrawal into himself and he became mute and unresponsive, but these periods were decreasing in frequency.

Brian is now in the fourth year. He tends to use words, both spoken and written, with great economy, managing to say as much in ten lines of writing as most others would say in a page. He has chosen Business Studies as one of his options so that he can continue to be involved with computers for word processing, data processing and spreadsheets. Another of his option choices was a surprise to his teachers and his parents – he decided to study drama. This has been most successful. He has taken part, with great confidence, in two public performances where many of the audience remarked on the clarity and fine quality of his speech.

QUESTIONS

1 Why is the computer such a good motivating tool?

2 Is it best to have a room full of computers which can be used periodically by each class or should we have a computer in each class-room?

3 How can we, or should we, ensure that the computer is serving the curriculum and not the curriculum serving the computer?

4 Is there transfer of learning from computer-assisted tasks to similar tasks in which the computer is not involved?

5 It has been suggested that word processing is one of the most effective language development tools. Is this true or is it rather a threat to hand-writing and to creative writing?

SUPPORTIVE INFORMATION AND MATERIAL

1 Useful programmes

COCKS, R., MASON, L. TWEDDLE, D. and WITHERS. F., *LET'S LEARN PHONICS.* A finely graded step-by-step programme covering a range of basic phonic skills (Malvern: Starnet Ltd).

MATSON, M., *GRANNY'S GARDEN.* An exciting adventure programme (4MAT Educational Software).

MESU, *PROMPT/WRITER*. A good programme for word processor using concept keyboard (Available from MESU).

MESU, *WINDOW*. A good programme to develop vocabulary and oral skills (Special Needs Software Centre, Manchester) (Available from MESU).

SMDP, *MICROSPECIAL PACK*. A suite of 25 programmes designed to teach life skills to young adults with special needs. Many programmes use the concept keyboard (London: William Collins Ltd. and Hill McGibbon).

SPEAR, L., *PEN DOWN*. An excellent word processing programme which produces print in a variety of fonts (Cambridge: Logotron).

Freely copiable BLUE FILE Software available from your LEA computer adviser.

HARRISON, D., *COMPACT*. (12 discs) An extensive suite of programmes operated via switches, concept keyboard or Micromike. Simple pictures are produced or moved by pressing switch etc. and can lead to verbal communication about various topics.

KEELING, R., *FRONT PAGE EXTRA*. (programme to produce a newspaper) (Newman College with MAPE).

MEP/BRISTOL UNIVERSITY, *CATCHUP*. (5 discs) Language development and early reading material for use with the concept keyboard. Especially useful for children with language difficulties and/or hearing impairment. Programmes range from activities for pre-reading levels to deductive skills for more able pupils.

MEP/LOUGHBOROUGH UNIVERSITY, *TALKING ABOUT NUMBERS*. (3 discs) A suite of number programmes starting with one to one correspondence, progressing to counting from one to ten. These should be used by an adult in discussion with a child, not by the child alone.

MOY, B. and BLAMIRES, M. *TRAY 2* and *INTRO TRAY*. A development of cloze procedure in which pupils build up a passage of text by guessing letters and predicting words and text. Teachers can control level of difficulty and can enter text which is suitable for individual pupils.

MUSHROOM SOFTWARE/MANCHESTER SEMERC, *MOVING IN*. An empty house is shown on the screen and the child can fill it with furniture, household objects and people by means of instructions from the concept keyboard or normal keyboard. Objects can be moved from one room to another and the people will perform tasks (have a bath, go to bed, play the piano etc.) and completed scene can be printed out.

NIXON, A. *ALAN NIXON KEYBOARD PROGRAMS*. 10 programmes using the keyboard or concept keyboard for: number or letter recognition games, snap games, mazes and puzzles.

NIXON, A. *ALAN NIXON SINGLE INPUT PROGRAMS*. 10 simple programmes (including matching games, 'odd-one-out', and building and animating pictures) requiring only a single input from a switch on a Micromike or the keyboard.

NIXON, A./SNSC/MANCHESTER/SEMERC. *LISTS*. A simple, jargon-free, database.

STRAKER, A. *et al*. *MALLORY*. (Crime detection programme with content free option) (Newman College with MAPE).

VINCENT, A. T. (1989) *New Technology, Disability and Special Educational Needs* (Coventry: FEU and Open University).

2 Useful addresses

Some suppliers of software and peripherals

Cambridge Microcomputer Centre,
153–4 East Road,
Cambridge, CB1 1DD

Carron Practicals,
Candover,
nr. Shrewsbury,
Shropshire, SY5 7AY.

Chalksoft Ltd,
PO Box 49,
Spalding,
Lincs, PE11 1NZ.

Collins Educational/Hill MacGibbon,
8 Grafton Street,
London, W1X 3LA.

Computer Concepts,
Gaddesden Place,
Hemel Hempstead,
Herts, HP2 6EX.

Hation,
'Linden Lea',
Rock Park,
Barnstaple,
Devon,
EX32 9AQ.

Interface Designs,
12 East Meads,
Oslow Village,
Guildford,
Surrey, GU2 5SP.

Jessop Microelectronics Ltd.,
Unit 5,
7 Long Street,
London, E2 8HN.

Logotron Ltd.,
Dales Brewery,
Gwydir St.,
Cambridge, CB1 2LJ.

Possum Controls Ltd.,
Middlegreen Trading Estate,
Middlegreen Road,
Langley,
Slough,
Berks, SL3 6DF.

Sherston Software,
Swan Burton,
Sherston,
Malmesbury,
Wilts., SN16 01H.

Special Access Systems Ltd.,
4 Benson Place,
Oxford, OX2 6QH.

Speech Systems Ltd,
Unit 8 Enterprise Row,
Rangemoor Road,
London, N15 4NG.

Star Microterminals Ltd,
22 Hyde Street,
Winchester,
Hampshire,
SO23 7DR.

Starnet Ltd,
PO Box 21,
Malvern,
WR14 2DX.

The Photonic Wand Company,
12 Orchard Croft,
Guilden Sutton,
Chester, CH3 7SL.

3 Useful reading

BEHRMANN, M. (1985) *Handbook of Microcomputers in Special Education* (Windsor: NFER–Nelson).

BLOWS, M. (1987) Making the most of a Word Processor. *Primary Teaching and Micros*. Jan. 1987, pp. 24–7.

CHANDLER, D. and MARCUS, S. (1985) *Computers and Literacy* (Milton Keynes: Open University Press).

DYKE, R. (1986) *Using Word Processing Programmes to support Low Attainers* (MESU Occasional Paper).

EMAP *Learning to Cope*. Annual publication on Micro-electronics in Special Education. Educational Computing, Magazine Services Department, Priory Court, 30–32 Farringdon Lane, London EC1R 3AU.

GOLDENBERG, P. (1984) *Computers, Education and Special Needs*. (Reading: Addison-Wesley Publishing Co.).

HALL, J. and RHODES, V. (1986) *Microcomputers in Primary Schools*. Educational (London: Computing Unit, Kings College).

JAMES, J. (1987) A Project on Crime Detection Using Mallory Manor. *Print Run*. Autumn 1987 (Bristol: SEMERC) pp. 1–5.

MESU *briefing* sheets, available from LEA Special Needs/Microelectronics Co-ordinators, or from MESU (address above).

SCHENK, C., (1986) *Hands On : Hands Off*. (London: A. and C. Black).

TELFORD, J. (1987) The case for the computer, *School Computer User*, No. 2. pp. 17–23.

CASE STUDY 12

Wendy

A thirteen-year-old child in need of counselling

Reason for referral

Wendy (aged 13 years) was referred to the Schools' Counsellor by her Form Tutor at the beginning of the 2nd year because she continued to be so passive in the context of the classroom and socially withdrawn from her peer group. Her abilities were described as within the 'low average' range and no learning difficulties were apparent.

Background

It became evident in the counselling sessions that Wendy's home situation was emotionally volatile due to the death two months previously of her maternal grandmother. Her mother, as well as trying to cope with her own grief, was allowing herself to be used by her father in such a way that her children – Wendy, her sister (10 years) and brother (6 years) – and husband were all adversely affected by her diverted attention. Every morning Wendy's mother collected her father from his sheltered accommodation and took him to her own home. His constant need to play his deceased wife's favourite records and to talk of his own possible pending suicide, together with requests for food, prevented Wendy's mother from completing her home-based assembly work. Usually he contrived still to be there when Wendy and her siblings returned home from school.

Wendy was well aware that she seemed to be her grandfather's favourite whereas he was exceedingly negative towards her brother; money was given to the two girls for sweets but none to the boy.

During the evenings, and usually at mealtimes, the grandfather used to tele phone and demand to speak to Wendy's mother: weekends he also spent time with the family.

Wendy knew that her grandfather had a medical disability but that he was still capable of driving his own car.

Client concerns

(a) Awareness of her mother's own depression.

(b)   Burden of mother's sharing with her some of her anxieties.

(c)   Mother's irritability and seeming to 'take it out on me'.

(d)   Worry about her grandfather's unfair treatment of her brother, but also not wanting to upset her own relationship with him.

(e)   Realisation that her father was becoming impatient with the grandfather and less tolerant of her mother's response to the situation.

(f)   Fear that grandfather would commit suicide.

(g)   Her own grief at her grandmother's death.

Action (with the client's agreement)

(a)   In order to break the daily pattern there seemed to be a need for her mother to find work outside the home. The situation was discussed with the Headmaster who, in turn, persuaded the school cook to offer Wendy's mother a temporary relief position in the school kitchen. She proved to be rather slow but was kept on, and was therefore no longer available all day for her father.

(b)   The Counsellor contacted 'CRUSE' who were prepared to offer the mother counselling if she telephoned the bereavement counselling service herself. The Counsellor had a frank discussion with Wendy's mother on the telephone during which she accepted her own need for help. She agreed to telephone CRUSE immediately so that she could speak to the counsellor who was aware of her situation. Wendy's mother was visited several times by a CRUSE counsellor and future help is available as required.

(c)   The Counsellor gave the Head of the Music Department some information about Wendy's family and she agreed to try to persuade the peripatetic clarinet teacher to reinstate Wendy's lessons. Wendy had expressed disappointment that for no obvious reason the lessons had stopped during the previous term.

       The lessons resumed and Wendy was encouraged to join both the school choir and orchestra. She has now performed in two public concerts.

(d)   Wendy was encouraged to join the St John's Ambulance Brigade which she currently attends regularly.

(e)   The situation was discussed with the family General Practitioner who agreed to try to persuade Wendy's grandfather to accept appropriate help. Unfortunately, when Wendy's mother finally succeeded in getting him to see the doctor he was unforthcoming about his feelings and behaviour.

(f)   On-going counselling should continue for Wendy.

(g)   A notice was put up in the staffroom asking the staff to be as positive as possible towards Wendy because of 'some family problems'.

QUESTIONS

1   Was a job outside the home the most important need for Wendy's mother, or was there an alternative strategy?

2   How might Wendy benefit from her mother's involvement with CRUSE and how efficient are such voluntary schemes in your opinion?

3   Why did the Counsellor give the Head of Music some details about Wendy's home situation, and does that have a wider message?

4   What information could be passed on to others without endangering the concept of confidentiality?

5   Was it wise to encourage Wendy to recommence clarinet lessons, partake in the school musical activities and join in out of school activity, or was this 'managing' her unduly?

6   What help would you consider to be appropriate for Wendy's grandfather?

7   Why was on-going counselling necessary for Wendy?

SUPPORTIVE INFORMATION AND MATERIAL

1   Some definitions of counselling

(a)   *An English Dictionary*

Counsel:
- To counsel a person: to give or offer (him counsel or advice).
- To give or offer counsel or advice.
- To counsel a thing: to advise its adoption or doing; to recommend (a plan, suggestion, etc.).
- To ask counsel of, to consult (obsolete).
- (Reflexive) to take counsel with oneself; to consider (obsolete).
- (Intransitive) to take counsel with others; to consult (obsolete).

Counsellor:
- One who counsels or advises: an adviser.

- An official counsellor; an adviser of the sovereign, a member of the King's Council. In this sense spelt since sixteenth century councillor.

- (More fully counsellor at law). One whose profession is to give legal advice to clients, and conduct their cases in court; a counselling lawyer, a barrister or advocate, archaic English use, still used in Ireland. In some of the United States, an attorney admitted to practise in all the courts.

- One who consults or asks counsel (obsolete, rare). Shakespeare, *Measure for Measure*: 'Good counsellors lacke no clients'.

(b)   *An American Dictionary*
Counsel:

- A mutual exchange of ideas, opinions etc.; discussion and deliberation.

- (i)   Advice resulting from such an exchange.
  (ii)   Any advice.

- (i)   Lawyer or group of lawyers giving advice about legal matters and representing clients in court.
  (ii)   Anyone whose advice is sought, consultant.

- Intention or resolution; purpose (archaic).

- Wisdom or judgement (archaic).

- A confidential idea, plan etc.; secret (obsolete).

Transitive verb:

- To give advice to; advise.

- To urge the acceptance of (an action, plan, etc.), recommend – to give or take advice. Keep one's own counsel – to keep one's thoughts, plans, etc. to oneself. Take counsel – to discuss and deliberate, exchange advice, opinions etc.

Counselor, counsellor:

- a person who counsels, adviser.

- a legal adviser, as of an embassy or legation.

- a lawyer, especially one who conducts cases in court: in full counsellor-at-law.

- a person in charge of a group of children at a camp.

(c)   A recent addition to an English dictionary includes the following definitions of counselling: 'The giving of advice on personal, social, psychological etc. problems as an occupation'. Counsellor is defined as 'One who specialises in counselling'.

(d) Personal counselling is characterised by:
  • Lack of pressure from the counsellor
  • Acceptance of a valid difficulty
  • Clarification of meaning for the client
  • A recognition of the validity of feeling
  • A tolerance of conflict
  • Personal acceptance

  J.H. Wallis (1973) *Personal Counselling* (Hemel Hempstead: Allen and Unwin).

(e) 'Basically and essentially all the practitioners of couselling have a common origin and a common aim: their common ancestor is the giver of spiritual solace and their common aim is health, sanity and a state of unspecified virtue, even a state of grace, or merely a return to the virtues of community adjustment . . . Above all, all counselling procedures share a method: they are all "Talking cures, semantic exercises, they all attempt treatment through clarification of subjective experience and meanings".'

  Paul Halmos (1965) *The Faith of the Counsellors* (London: Constable) pp. 2–3.

(f) 'Counselling is a very highly skilled job. It means helping people to understand their own motives and reasons for action so that they can come to their own conclusions about what they will do and how they can do it; it means helping them to understand their feelings, emotions and behaviour, it means enabling them to define their needs and discover what resources are available to them to meet these; it means helping them to work out the best ways of making and maintaining satisfactory relationships with others.'

  George Lovel, *The Youth Worker as First-Aid Counsellor in Impromptu Situations* (Peterborough: Chester House Publications).

(g) *School counselling*:
  '. . . an enabling process, designed to help an individual come to terms with his life as it is and ultimately to grow to greater maturity through learning to take responsibility and to make decisions for himself.' (p. 10)

  '. . . results from a relationship between two people, one needing an opportunity of talking over his problems, the other having the sensitivity and maturity thoroughly to appreciate the uncertainties and conflicts involved, and having the necessary knowledge and skills to enable a solution or at least some accommodation to the difficulty to be reached.' (para. 2.11)

  School Counselling (1970) (London: National Association for Mental Health).

(h) '(i) A face-to-face, person-in-person relationship in which a person(s) (the client) seeks the help of or seeks to effectively communicate with another person (the counsellor).

(ii) A relationship characterised by mutual respect, effective communications, genuine and complete acceptance of the client by the counsellor, and concentration on the needs, problems and feelings of the client.

(iii) A unique relationship that brings about permissiveness which encourages complete freedom of thought and expression of feelings on the part of the client.

(iv) An open-ended relationship in which the responsibility for the outcomes rests primarily with the client, not with the counsellor.

(v) A relationship which facilitates growth and change in the client, enabling the client to become more freely and fully functioning.

(vi) A relationship in which the client's desire for confidentiality is respected.

(vii) A professional service that calls for skills and attitudes on the part of the counsellor not usually possessed by a layman.

(viii) A professional service based upon a substantive rationale that reflects philosophical and psychological principles emanating from theoretical and empirical considerations of men, humane behaviour, and society.' (p. 139)

> A.V. Boy and G.J. Pine (1968) *The Counsellor in the schools*, (Boston: Houghton Mifflin) p. 139.

(i) '. . . an interview situation characterised by an absence of moralising, by sympathy without sentimentality, concern without interference and with no strings attached, where one person sets out to enable another to examine confusion in thinking and feeling, reach his own diagnosis and perhaps formulate workable plans for the immediate or even more distant future.'

> Patrick Hughes (1971) *Guidance and Counselling in Schools* (Oxford: Pergamon) p. 33.

(j) 'Counselling is a process of sharing not only behaviour' (i.e. what is observed) 'but experience' (what is hidden), 'the creation of a relationship of such trust and confidence that the defensive walls we erect around ourselves are dismantled stone by stone.' (p. 36)

> Ken Williams (1973) *The School Counsellor* (London: Methuen) p. 36.

(k) 'Counselling can be defined very widely as any professional activity which makes for good communication between people.'
More narrowly, 'Counselling . . . is a relationship between two people where one person (the client) is aware of a problem and of the need to talk it over with another (the counsellor).' (p. 21)

'Individual counselling in schools can be defined as a way of offering an opportunity to the young person to experience a one-to-one relationship which is accepting and tolerant yet relatively free from moralising, directing, advising or judging. In this way the hope is that enough understanding will be gained of themselves so that they can stand on their own feet without support.' (pp. 103–4)

H.J. Taylor (1971) *School Counselling* (Basingstoke: Macmillan)

2 Listening

(a) Listening is an art, a skill and a discipline. It requires control – intellectual, emotional and behavioural. The individual must understand what is involved in listening and in developing the necessary self-mastery to be silent and listen.

(b) Listening obviously is based on hearing and understanding of what others say to us. Hearing becomes listening only when we pay attention to what is said and follow it very closely.

(c) We should try to create a situation in which people can
   - discuss frankly matters which are important to them
   - give without embarrassment as much information as possible
   - gain insight and understanding of their problems as they talk them out
   - try to see the causes and reasons for their problems
   - work out for themselves what action to take.

(d) Responses may be as follows:
Clarifying
   (i) To get at additional facts – 'Can you clarify this?'
   (ii) To help him explore all sides of – 'Do you mean this . . .?' of a problem
   (iii) To check our meaning and interpretation with his – 'Is this the problem as you see it now . . .?'
   (iv) To show you are listening and that you understand what he is saying. – 'As I understand it then . . .'

Neutral
   (i) To convey that you are listening and are interested – 'I see'
   (ii) To encourage him to talk – 'Uh-huh'
   – 'That's very interesting'
   – 'I understand'.

Collective
   (i) To show that you understand how he feels about what he is saying – 'You feel that . . .?'

(ii) To help him to evaluate his own feelings as expressed by someone else

– 'It was a shocking thing as you saw it . . .?'
– 'You felt you didn't get a fair show . . .?'

Summarising
(i) To bring the discussion into focus

– 'These are the key ideas you have expressed . . .?'

(ii) To serve as a spring board for further discussion

– 'If I understand how you feel about the situation . . .'.

3 Interviewing pupils

Normal problems in counselling include:
Puberty and adolescent status
Independence – standing alone
Emotions and self-control – moods
Sexuality and the opposite sex
Intelligence level and achievement
Physical – clumsiness and body image
Temporary worries and moods – self-consciousness
Relationships with relatives
Social competence and coping skills – self-consciousness
Relationships with contemporaries
Values and boundaries in personal life
Achievement and learning skills
Money and materialism
Jobs
Relationships with authority

4 Referral agencies and possible discussion group visitors

Educational psychologists
Psychiatrists
Medical Officers of the Health Authority
General medical practitioners
Remedial centre teachers
College of Education and University counsellors
Health Education Staff
Social Services Staff
Probation Staff
Police and Juvenile Bureau Staff
School nurses and health visitors
Parents and relatives
Citizens Advice Bureau Staff
Local councillors
Samaritans
Clergy and RE and moral education Teachers
Careers officers and teachers
Employers
Headteachers, advisers and curriculum development officers
Housing officers
Relate (Marriage Guidance Council) counsellors

Educational Welfare Officers	Councils for Social (or Voluntary)
Young People's Advisory Services	Service
Youth Workers	Councils for Alcoholism and Drug
Family Planning and Brook	Abuse
Centres	Diocesan Councils for Social Work
NSPCC	

5   There are well-known 'blocks' to careful listening

- 'Pre-occupied' listening (open ears, closed mind).
- Stereotyping and status prevent understanding.
- Physical conditions preclude attention.
- 'Wandering mind' and 'on-off' listening.
- Past experience and prejudices affect what we are hearing.
- Hostility and defensiveness put-up barriers.
- Personal anxieties and overwork.

Does anybody know what anybody really says?!
Most individuals think about four times as fast as the average person speaks. Thus, the listener has ¾ of a minute spare thinking time for each listening minute.

6   Useful reading

DAVID, K. and COWLEY, J. (1980) *Pastoral Care in schools and Colleges* (London: Edward Arnold).

DAVID, K. (1983) *Personal and Social Education in Secondary Schools* (London: Schools Council).

DEAN, H. and DEAN, M. (1981) *Counselling in a Troubled Society* (London: Unwin).

FURMAN, E. (1974) *A Child's Parent Dies* (Yale University Press).

GALLOWAY, D. (1978) *Teaching and Counselling* (Harlow: Longman).

HAMBLIN, D. (1978) *The Teacher and Pastoral Care* (Oxford: Blackwell).

HOLDEN, A. (1973) *Teachers as Counsellors* (London: Constable).

McNEIL TAYLOR, L. (1983) *Living with Loss* (London: Fontana).

ROGERS, C. (1971) *'On becoming a Person'* (London: Constable).

WARD, B. and HOUGHTON, J. (1987) *Good Grief – talking and learning about Loss and Death* (Good Grief Associates, 84 Ebury Street, London SW1).

WARDEN, W. (1983) *Grief Counselling and Grief Therapy* (London: Tavistock).

WYLNE, T. (1980) *Counselling Young People* (Leicester: National Youth Bureau).

A useful address
CRUSE,
Cruse House, 126 Sheen Road,
Richmond, Surrey, TW9 1UR.
Telephone 081 940 4818/9042.

Tommy

A route for a misfit

Tommy was sentenced to 4 months at a detention centre at the age of 19, for supplying cannabis to fellow members of a youth club, providing him with profitable pocket money. The cannabis was probably supplied to him by a distant relative who was employed at a dockyard in the south of England. A girl in the club informed her policeman brother and an arrest was made at the club late one evening. The club leader, a professional youth worker, had suspected what was going on, but had not been able to find clear proof. The youth leader had been co-operating with a drug squad sergeant on this matter.

Tommy's father died when he was seven years old, leaving the working mother with two boys and a younger daughter. The mother was a secretary, hard working and with a comfortable home in a council estate. The elder brother, four years older than Tommy, had been a bright and lively pupil at school, and had gained a full scholarship to a private school. This elder boy did well at 'O' level, modestly well at 'A' level, and went to a provincial university which he left after one year, to follow a successful career in a middle-grade civil service post, eventually marrying and bringing up a family.

The younger boy, Tommy, did not settle well at school and was referred to Child Guidance at age 9 for eneuresis. The mother was informed that he had a high intelligence, but was 'socially retarded'. It was expected that he would do well as he grew older. He went at the age of 11 to a selective Secondary School, and after a good first year, slowly went downhill academically and socially. Outside school he mixed with a lively and troublesome gang of friends who were unpopular locally, and 'watched' by the police.

The school had a carefully planned and effective pastoral system, but failed to do much with Tommy, excluding him frequently from class, and complaining to the mother on several occasions. His behaviour deteriorated markedly in the third year, and he threatened a woman teacher with a knife after a classroom incident where he was leading the class in mocking the teacher.

After this incident the local authority, on the urging of the Headmaster, recommended Tommy for a placement in a residential school, because of his disturbed behaviour. He refused to go, and was supported in this by his mother who felt it was better to keep him at home. His behaviour to his mother appeared to give no particular cause for concern. His dealings with his brother were minimal until his brother left home, and remained distant afterwards. His relations with his young sister were good, and he was generous and caring for her. She, like her mother, was quiet and unassertive, and stable in temperament.

He next went, at his own request, to a non-selective school, quietened down, and left at age 16 with some modest 'O' level passes. After a variety of undemanding casual jobs, he decided that society and his mother could keep him. He resumed his friendship with some of his former troublesome gang of friends and attempted to assert himself as a leader of the youngsters in the youth club, which was a large one run by the local authority.

QUESTIONS

1 At what point in Tommy's life could better action have been taken in his personal development?

2 How would one summarise his background in assessing future guidance?

3 Should his career of trouble have been expected, in assessing his background?

4 Did the school system fail him, or was his story to be expected?

SUPPORTIVE INFORMATION AND MATERIAL

1 The Youth Service

The National Advisory Council for the Youth Service in 'A Consultation Paper on a strategy to raise the effectiveness of the Youth Service' (DES, 1988) states:

> The Youth Service is diverse and complex. It offers to several million young people a wide range of opportunities for their personal and social development. These opportunities include: youth clubs; school-based youth centres; uniformed organisation; residential centres; specialised centres e.g. in the arts, and in sport. In recent years there has been diversification into special projects for young women, for young people who are unemployed, for young people from different ethnic communities. "Detached" or "outreach" workers seek to promote contact with young people not in formal organisations. Specialised agencies offer counselling, advice and befriending services e.g. on youngsters' relationships difficulties, on drug misuse, on sexual matters or on their housing needs.
>
> Over the past 20 years the Youth Service has come to adopt the phrase 'social education' to explain its underlying purpose and define its central task. The aim of social education is to enable persons as individuals and

as members of their communities to take charge of their personal lives and play a responsible role in the life of the communities so that they may be able to make decisions for themselves and have a part in the decision-making processes of the community. Youth work helps young people to become critically conscious of themselves and others including the wider society and to take steps to improve their situation. Where the educational task of youth workers differs from much teaching in schools or colleges is that the interventions to foster the intended skills often cannot be planned for opportunities frequently have to be taken "on the wing" in a variety of social or recreational contexts established by youth service in order to enable productive contact with as many young people as possible. At some stage in their lives over 90% of young people are associated in some way with the variety of offerings which we have come to know as the Youth Service, even if this term has yet to secure a clear definition in the popular imagination.

Youth work has always relied on responding to young people as and when they present themselves but it can be asked whether those who would benefit most from social education are encouraged to present themselves and whether their most significant needs would be addressed if they did. There has also always been a commitment in principle if not always in practice to enable young people using the Youth Service to exercise increasing control over decision-making and to devise and lead activity. Young people come on their own terms and on matters which concern them – which may or may not be confined by notions of "education". In consequence, youth workers and young poeple may co-operate in securing young people's welfare rights or a roof over their heads or reducing their alcohol misuse or speaking out about their need for jobs . . . Youth Service's particular stance of trying to work with how young people see the world often marks it off from other agencies – schools, social work, the family, commercial entertainment.

2 Drugs

(a)   *The Health Education Authority* (78 New Oxford Street, London WC1A 1AH. Telephone 071 631 0930) publish a resource list of books, pamphlets, and leaflets, posters and charts, films and videos, film strips/slides/tapes/film loops, and packs.

(b)   *Health Education Officers* of District Health Authorities can provide resources, talks and training opportunities.

(c)   *The Teacher's Advisory Council for Alcohol and Drug Education* (TACADE) (Furness House, Trafford Road, Salford, M5 2XJ. Telephone 061 848 0351) can provide resources, speakers and training opportunities, and publish a regular 'Monitor' publication.

(d) *The Institute for the Study of Drug Dependence* (ISD), (1–4 Hatton Place, Hatton Garden, London, EC1N 8ND. Telephone 071 430 1991) provide research materials and resources.

3 Pastoral care in schools – a checklist for discussion   P

(a) Pastoral care should be *positive, planned* and *professional*.

(b) It is *not*:
- primarily disciplinary
- intended to cover up school faults
- an occasional happening
- just welfare
- only intended to remedy deficiencies in individual pupils.

(c) It *is*:
- about learning processes
- about creating a sense of order and clarity
- creating routines for diagnosing problems
- reviewing action taken and results obtained
- continuous through a pupil's career in a school
- for all children, not a few
- a partnership with parents
- not only intuitive and accidental
- preventive.

(d) It includes:
- the quality of the leadership of the school
- the quality of staff relationships
- pastoral appointments and status
- a strong emphasis on a team approach
- in each pastoral team the skills of:
  - counselling
  - group discussion
  - learning and study methods
  - human development
  - tutorial work.
- liaison with other agencies, and referral systems
- good communication within the school and planned systems
- record-keeping and reports
- welfare arrangements

- order, discipline and attendance supervision
- social and leisure education
- standards and achievement in learning
- assessing the effect of the timetable and curriculum on individuals and groups of pupils
- assessing the effect of school rituals in individuals and groups
- regular evaluation of all aspects of the school.

4 Discussion notes on self-confidence and achievement

(a) Samuel Smiles 'Self Help' (1850):

'We often discover what *will* do by finding out what will *not* do; and probably he who never made a mistake never made a discovery'.

(b) There are many books and articles on building self-confidence; Dale Carnegie's early 'How to make friends and influence people' (1950) was a best seller. In an increasingly complex and demanding society people are seeking the keys to presenting themselves satisfactorily, in gaining acceptance, and in developing a sense of belonging in a more anonymous environment.

(c) Society used to be fairly clearly stratified by class. There was confidence in knowing one's class setting, behaviour, and expectations, and the next class mode could be learned. Social classes are more homogenous and fluid now, and establishing one's identity and worth is more confusing.

(d) Could these questions, if answered honestly, be the start of improving self-confidence:

Do you believe you are unlucky? Do you believe people dislike you, talk about you? When strangers look at you do you presume laughter? Do you constantly criticise others? And complain? Are you shy, embarrassed, afraid?

(e) Can we then consider:
   (i)   Few *need* feel lack of confidence *in reality*.
   (ii) In truth *everyone* is vulnerable to doubts, even the most confident-looking person.
   (iii) Realise the *ordinariness* of others.
         Aldous Huxley suggested: 'imagine the person you are in awe of sitting in a tin bath, too small for him, trying to wash his feet'.
   (iv) Look for your *talents*, however modest, and emphasise them. Reward your *successes* in some way, and advertise them if necessary.
   (v)   Consider whether your mistakes and errors do in fact *matter*, when you consider them without emotion.

(vi) Consider what you *like* doing, not what you think you ought to like doing. If it does not hurt others or yourself why not do what *you* like?

(vii) Give attention to your *appearance*, clothes, manners.

(viii) *Be honest* and seek help from others who could guide you. Perhaps they could help you:

- to *set goals for yourself*, specific behaviours, objectives, targets in which you have a reasonable chance of success.
- To learn how to *use mistakes constructively*.
- To learn social and *co-operative skills*, including conversation.
- To practise *perseverance*, and to begin *planning ahead*.
- To learn of *supportive systems*, and perhaps of *group counselling*.

(f) Can we discuss these themes with children? At what age? Is it suitable for group discussions, or individual counselling?

5   Differing views on education – themes for discussion

(a) School feels like this to children; it is a place where *they* make you go and where *they* tell you to do things and where *they* try to make your life unpleasant if you don't do them or don't do them right.

John Holt, *How Children Fail*

(b) I believe that to improve anything by authority is wrong. The child should not do anything until he comes to the opinion – his own opinion – that it should be done.

Neill Summerhill

(c) The world is a noisy, chaotic and restless place, yet in school we see the same lack of quiet encouraged. It is putting a great strain on young children to leave them constantly to make decisions with rarely any time in the day when they are quiet and listening.

C.M. Johnson, *Black Papers*

(d) 'I see you, and you see me. I experience you and you experience me. I see your behaviour, and you see my behaviour. But I do not and never have and never will see your *experience* of me. I cannot experience your experience. You cannot experience my experience. We are both invisible men. All men are invisible to one another.'

R.D. Laing, *The Politics of Experience*

(e) 'Every individual biography is an episode within the history of society which both precedes and survives it . . . What is more, it is within society, and as a result of social processes, that the individual becomes a person, that he attains and holds on to an identity and that he carries out the various projects that constitute his life. ' 'Men must talk about themselves until they know themselves.'

Berger and Luckman, *The Social Construction of Reality*

(f)   Give your scholar no verbal lessons; he should be taught by experience alone.

J.J. Rousseau

(g)   What we have here (in suggested reforms) is the dream of the millenium, in which all men work together in a spirit of harmony, co-operation and brotherly love. It is a fantasy that has bewitched small groups of cranks throughout history. But the real world is competitive and likely to remain so . . . Children have to be educated for the real world and this involves training for competition as well as for co-operation.

Richard Lynn, *Black Papers*

(h)   *Bertrand Russell* was asked to define the essence of a liberal attitude. He suggested the following:

1   Do not feel absolutely certain of anything.
2   Do not think it worthwhile to proceed by concealing evidence, for the evidence is sure to come to light.
3   Never try to discourage thinking, for you are sure to succeed.
4   When you meet with opposition, even if it should be from your husband or your children, endeavour to overcome it by argument and not by authority, for a victory dependent upon authority is unreal and illusory.
5   Have no respect for the authority of others, for there are always contrary authorities to be found.
6   Do not suppress opinions you think pernicious, for if you do the opinions will suppress you.
7   Do not fear to be eccentric in opinion, for every opinion now accepted was once eccentric.
8   Find more pleasure in intelligent dissent than in passive agreement, for if you value intelligence as you should, the former implies a deeper agreement than the latter.
9   Be scrupulously truthful, even if the truth is inconvenient, for it is more inconvenient when you try to conceal it.
10   Do not feel envious of the happiness of those who live in a fool's paradise, for only a fool will think that it is happiness.

6   Personal and social development of young people – useful reading

ACRES, D. (1984) *Examinations without Anxiety* (Stoke-on-Trent: Deanhouse).
ASSESSMENT OF PERFORMANCE UNIT (1981) Personal and Social Development, (London: DES).

BARNETT, C *et al.* (1985) *Learning Through Experience* (London: Macmillan).

BELL, L. and MAHER, P. (1986) *Leading a Pastoral Team* (Oxford: Basil Blackwell).

BEST, R., JARVIS, C. and RIBBINS, P. (1980) *Perspectives on Pastoral Care* (London: Heinemann Educational).

BLACKBURN, K. (1978) *The Tutor* (London: Heinemann Educational).

BLACKBURN, K. (1983) *Head of House, Head of Year* (London: Heinemann Educational).

BOLAM, R and MEDLOCK, D. (1985) *Active Tutorial Work: Training and Dissemination: an Evaluation* (Oxford: Basil Blackwell for Health Education Council).

BOND, T. (1986) *Games for Social and Life Skills* (London: Hutchinson).

BRANDES, D. and GINNIS, P. (1986) *A Handbook of Student-centred Learning* (Oxford: Basil Blackwell).

BRANDES, D and PHILIPS, H. (1981) *Gamesters Handbook, Book 1* (London: Hutchinson).

BRANDES, D. (1982) *Gamesters Handbook Two* (London: Hutchinson).

BRAUN, D. and EISENSTADT, N. (1986) *Family Lifestyles* (Milton Keynes: Open University Press).

BRAUN, D. and EISENSTADT, N. (1985) *Childhood* (Milton Keynes: Open University Press).

BROWN, C., HARBER, C. and STRIVENS, J. (eds.) (1986) *Social Education: Principles and Practice* (Lewes: Falmer Press).

BULMAN, L. and JENKINS, D. (1986) *The Pastoral Curriculum* (Oxford: Basil Blackwell).

BUTLER, B. and ELLIOTT, D. (1985) *Teaching and Learning for Practice* (Aldershot: Gower Publishing Co.).

BUTTERWORTH, C. and MACDONALD, M. (1985) *Teaching Social Education and Communication: A Practical Handbook* (London: Hutchinson).

BUTTON, L. (1982) *Group Tutoring for the Form Teacher. Books 1 and 2* (London: Hodder and Stoughton).

CLEATON, D.R. (1985) *Exercises in Social and Personal Education* (Richmond: Careers Consultants Ltd).

CLEMETT, T. and PEARCE, J. (1986) *The Evaluation of Pastoral Care* (Oxford: Basil Blackwell).

COHEN, L. and COHEN, A. (eds) (1987) *Disruptive Behaviour: A Source Book for Teachers* (London: Harper and Row).

COLES, M. and WHITE, C. (1985) *Strategies for Studying* (Glasgow: Collins).

COLLINS, N. (1986) *New Teaching Skills* (Oxford: Oxford University Press).

DAVID, K. (1983) *Personal and Social Education in Secondary Schools* (London: Longman for Schools Council).

DAVID, K. and WILLIAMS, T. (eds.) (1987) *Health Education in Schools* (2nd Edition) (London: Harper and Row).

DAVIES, G.T. (1986) *A First Year Tutorial Handbook* (Oxford: Basil Blackwell).

DES (1979) *Aspects of Secondary Education in England* (London: HMSO).

DES (1980) *A view of the Curriculum* (London: HMSO).

DES (1983) *Learning Out of Doors* (London: HMSO).

DES (1985) *Better Schools* (London: HMSO).

DIXON, H. and MULLINAR, G. (1983) *Taught not Caught! Strategies for Sex Education* (Wisbech: Learning Development Aids).

DOCKING, J.W. (1987) *Control and Discipline in Schools: Perspectives and Approaches (2nd Edition)* (London: Harper and Row).

DOUGLAS, T. (1983) *Groups* (London: Tavistock).

DYSON, S. and SCIROM, T. (1986) *Greater Expectations* (Exeter: RMEP).

ELLIS, D and WHITTINGTON, D. (1982) *New Directions in Social Skill Training,* (Beckenham: Croom Helm).

FOSTER, J. (1985–7) *Lifelines: a Social and Personal Development Course* (5 books) (Glasgow: Collins).

FURTHER EDUCATION CURRICULUM REVIEW AND DEVELOPMENT UNIT (FEU) (1980) *Beyond Coping: Some Approaches to Social Education* (London: FEU).

FURTHER EDUCATION CURRICULUM REVIEW AND DEVELOPMENT UNIT (FEU) (1982) *Developing Social and Life Skills: Strategies for Tutors* (London: FEU).

FURTHER EDUCATION CURRICULUM REVIEW AND DEVELOPMENT UNIT (FEU) (1982) *Tutoring* (London: NICEC/FEU).

FURTHER EDUCATION CURRICULUM REVIEW AND DEVELOPMENT UNIT (FEU) (1986) *Developing Social and Life Skills* (London: FEU).

GAMMAGE, P. (1982) *Children and Schooling: Issues in Childhood Socialisation* (London: George Allen and Unwin).

GREENWOOD, W. (ed.) (1986) *Perspectives on Religious Education and Personal and Social Education* (Isleworth: Christian Education Movement).

GRUNSELL, R. (1985) *Finding Answers to Disruption: Discussion Exercises for Secondary Teachers* (London: SCDC Publication–Longman).

HAMBLIN, D.H. (1974) *The teacher and counselling* (Oxford: Basil Blackwell).

HAMBLIN, D.H. (1977) *The teacher and pastoral care* (Oxford: Basil Blackwell).

HAMBLIN, D.H. (1981) *Problems and practice of pastoral care* (Oxford: Basil Blackwell).

HAMBLIN, D.H. (1981) *Teaching Study Skills* (Oxford: Basil Blackwell).

HAMBLIN, D.H. (1983) *Guidance for the 16-19 age group* (Oxford: Basil Blackwell).

HAMBLIN, D.H. (1984) *Pastoral Care: a Training Manual* (Oxford: Basil Blackwell).

HAMBLIN, D.H. (1986) *A Pastoral Programme* (Oxford: Basil Blackwell).

HARGREAVES, A. (1986) *Establishing Social Education* (Oxford: Basil Blackwell).

HARGREAVES, D.H. (1972) *Interpersonal Relations and Education* (London: Routledge and Kegan Paul).

HARGREAVES, D.H. (1982) *The Challenge for the Comprehensive School* (London: Routledge and Kegan Paul).

HMI (1985) *The Curriculum From 5 to 16, Curriculum Matters 2* (London: HMSO).

HMI (1986) *Health Education from 5 to 16, Curriculum Matters series*, 6 (London: HMSO).

HOPSON, B. and SCALLY, M. (1980) *Lifeskills Teaching Programmes, Numbers 1, 2 and 3* (Leeds: Lifeskills Associates).

HOPSON, B. (1981) *Lifeskills Teaching* (Maidenhead: McGraw Hill).

HOPSON, B. and SCALLY, M. (1984) *Build Your Own Rainbow* (Leeds: Lifeskills Associates).

HUMPHRIES, W.E., MEAGER, J.E. *et al*. (1986) *Decision Making: a Political Education Pack* (London: Arnold).

HUNT, S. and HILTON, J. (1975) *Individual Development and Social Experience* (Hemel Hempstead: George Allen and Unwin).

JAQUES, D. (1984) *Learning in Groups* (Beckenham: Croom Helm).

JONES, T. and PALMER, K. (1986) *In Other People's Shoes: The Use of Role-Play in Personal, Social and Moral Education* (Exeter: RMEP).

LANCASHIRE COUNTY COUNCIL (1978–83) Active Tutorial Work (six books in series),
Book 1 – The first year
Book 2 – The second year
Book 3 – The third year
Book 4 – The fourth year
Book 5 – The fifth year
Book 6 – Sixteen to nineteen
(Resource packs for Books 1–5 available)
(Oxford: Basil Blackwell).

LANG, P. and MARLAND, M. (eds) (1985) *New Directions in Pastoral Care* (Oxford: Basil Blackwell).

LAWTON, A. (1985) *Parents and Teenagers* (London: Unwin Paperbacks).

LEECH, N. and WOOSTER, A.D. (1986) *Personal and Social Skills: a Practical Approach for the Classroom* (Nottingham University, RMEP).

MARLAND, M. (1978) *Pastoral Care* (London: Heinemann Educational).

MARLAND, M. (1983) *Sex Differentiation and Schools*, (Tadworth: Heinemann).

MCGUINESS, J.B. (1982) *Planned Pastoral Care* (London: McGraw-Hill).

MCGUIRE, J. and PRIESTLEY, P. (1981) *Life After School: A Social Skills Curriculum* (Oxford: Pergamon).

MCPHAIL, P., UNGOED-THOMAS, J. and CHAPMAN, H. (1972) *Moral Education in the Secondary School* (York: Longman for Schools Council).

MCPHAIL, P. (1982) *Social and Moral Education* (Oxford: Basil Blackwell).

MORGAN, J. (1984–6) *Tutor Group Worksheets* (Years 1, 2, 3 and 4) (Oxford: Basil Blackwell).

PRIESTLEY, P. *et al*. (1978) *Social Skills and Personal Problem-Solving*, (London: Tavistock).

PRING, R. (1984) *Personal and Social Education in the Curriculum* (London: Hodder and Stoughton).

RAYMOND, J. (1985) *Implementing Pastoral Care in Schools* (London: Croom Helm).

RICE, W. (1981) *Informal Methods in Health and Social Education* (Manchester: TACADE).

RUTTER, M., et al. (1979) *Fifteen Thousand Hours* (Shepton Mallet: Open Books).

SCHOOLS COUNCIL (1976) *Health Education in Secondary Schools: Working Paper 57* (London: Methuen).

SCHOOLS COUNCIL (1981) *The Practical Curriculum, Working Paper 70* (London: Methuen).

SCHOOLS COUNCIL (1984) *Developing Health Education, Health Education 13–18 project* (London: Forbes publications).

SCRIMSHAW, P. (1981) *Community Service, Social Education and the Curriculum* (London: Hodder and Stoughton).

SETTLE, D. and WISE, C. (1986) *Choices: Methods and Materials for Personal and Social Education* (Oxford: Basil Blackwell).

SINGER, E. and JOHNSON, R. (1985) *Personal Development: a Personal Effectiveness. Resource Pack* (Sheffield: COIC).

SMITH, P. (1986) *Simulations for Careers and Life Skills* (London: Hutchinson).

STRADLING, R. et al. (1984) *Teaching Controversial Issues* (London: Arnold).

STRADLING, R. (1986) *Political Education: A Handbook for Teachers* (London: Arnold).

SWANN REPORT (1985) *Education for All. The report of the committee of inquiry into the education of children from ethnic minority groups* (London: HMSO).

TABBERER, R. and ALLMAN, J. (1983) *Introducing Study Skills: an Appraisal of Initiatives at 16+* (Windsor: NFER–Nelson).

THACKER, J. (1982) *Steps to Success: an Interpersonal Problem-solving Approach for Children* (Windsor: NFER–Nelson).

THOMAS, P. (1984) *New Directions* (Amersham: Hulton Educational).

WAKEMAN, B. (1984) *Personal, Social and Moral Education* (Tring: Lion Publishing).

WARNOCK REPORT (1978) *Special Educational Needs Report of the Committee of Enquiry into the Education of Handicapped Children and Young People* (London: HMSO).

WENT, D. (1985) *Sex Education: Some Guidelines for Teachers* (London: Bell and Hyman).

WHITE R, and BROCKINGTON, D. (1983) *Tales Out of School* (London: Routledge and Kegan Paul).

WHYLD, J. (ed.) (1983) *Sexism in the Secondary Curriculum* (London: Harper and Row).

WILCOX, B. et al. (1984) *The Preparation for Life Curriculum* (Beckenham: Croom Helm).

CASE STUDY 14

Savas

*Low self-esteem in a
Secondary School child*

Savas's mother had been raised as a white Protestant in a middle-class rural area, while his father was a Muslim of Middle Eastern origin, who had emigrated to England two years before the marriage. The cultural backgrounds of the two parents were diverse. Father was learning English, which was spoken in the home. The first child of the family had been a girl, who had shown a flair for languages, and had achieved excellent school reports. Savas's arrival had been the fulfilment of his father's desire for 'a son'. Savas did not exhibit the flair for language shown by his sister, nor did his scholastic achievements match hers. Both parents were aware of the boy in terms of his 'failure' to equal his sister.

Comparisons were made by his Infant School and his first Junior School regarding his sister's excellence and his limitations. Savas's response was to exhibit disruptive behaviour both in and out of the classroom. His academic achievements were poor; however, he was praised both verbally and in each annual report for his art work. Father did not recognise art as an important area and decried any achievements made in this area. Open Days had become a problem to Savas's mother, who was always protective of him, and made allowances for him. Father did not attend Open Days, and proved to be a strict authoritarian, with unrealistic expectations for his son. Savas was not allowed to 'play out' with friends or bring friends home, because he had to concentrate on his studies. His social skills were therefore limited.

Savas entered his Secondary School having been to four primary schools. His first Church of England Infant School was in a middle-class semi-rural area. He subsequently went to the Church of England Junior School, which was situated approximately a mile from the Infant School, there being little liaison between the two. His sister had attended both schools two years earlier. When he was eight his family moved to an inner-city location and he attended the local Junior School; he, along with four others, were the only pupils having English as a first language in his class of 34. His academic achievements were limited and his father, who was developing his own understanding of the English Language felt that his son should be in a predominantly white English-speaking school. Thus his last two years of primary school were spent in a fee-paying private school. The high expectations of his father, as well as the school, proved unrealistic, and Savas exhibited disruptive behaviour culminating with a situation involving the police. He was subsequently expelled from the school.

Savas joined his Community Comprehensive School with limited achievements in Maths and English. His written work was very poor. He spoke about himself in very negative terms, saying that he was a 'div' and did not care if he could not do the work. He acknowledged that he had no friends. The pastoral system at the school allowed a period each week to be spent with personal tutors. Mr Hinge, Savas's personal tutor, who had taken a course in Personal, Social and Health Education, noted Savas's interest and ability in Art. Simultaneously, the PE master recognised Savas's ability in sport. It was suggested that he join the football team and attend art evening classes. He subsequently made friends with his peers.

Links were made with the parents via the personal tutor, and the importance of recognising Savas's achievements rather than his failures was outlined. Father still saw his son as a failure, mother tried to make excuses for him, blaming the school and the location. Nevertheless, both parents were prepared to listen to the tutor, as they appeared to be unable to think of ways of improving Savas's behaviour themselves and were worried that Savas might be expelled again. They agreed to try to see his achievements in terms of progression rather than in comparison to his sister's achievements. Father was still suspect of the Art bias; he did not consider it 'manly' enough for his son, whom he expected to become a doctor or a lawyer; however, he stated that sport was certainly an achievement worthy of a boy.

On reaching his third year at the Community Comprehensive School, Savas had become a member of the school football and rugby teams. He excelled in athletics and had won many school-based prizes for his artistic achievements. He exhibited signs of leadership and had become a popular member of the class. His academic achievements, however, still showed limited positive improvement. His disruptive behaviour had subsided, so too had his ability always to find an excuse for his misbehaviour. Mother recognised that she could no longer make excuses for her son while Father now saw his son as a potential football player for Liverpool! Finally, at the age of 14, Savas was beginning to feel part of the school society.

After the initial meeting with the personal tutor, both parents have become active members of the community aspects of the school, attending evening classes and becoming members of the 'Fund Raising' Committee.

SUPPORTIVE INFORMATION AND MATERIAL

1 Self-concept

(a) Self-concept is the picture, image, or view that an individual has of him or herself. It is, first, an awareness of the self as an individual, as a dis-

QUESTIONS

1   Did the father's unrealistic expectations and the mother's excuses, in fact, produce a low self-concept and an external locus of control in Savas?

2   How could earlier liaison between home and school have prevented the situation arising where Savas was seen in terms of his 'failures'?

3   In response to the National Curriculum, could attainment targets in the three core areas of Language, Science and Mathematics reinforce a low self-concept in a child with limited academic achievement?

4   How could the school be aware of the parents' expectations of the system, so that the child is not the centre of a situation which is giving 'mixed messages'? The school was praising artistic achievement while the home was calling it 'sissy'. Also the father was expecting Savas to become a doctor or a lawyer while the school was aware of his limited academic achievements.

5   What was the 'turning point' for Savas?

6   Should *every* teacher follow a course in Personal, Social and Health Education?

7   How should the affective history of the learner (i.e. interests, attitudes, motivations, self-concept and personality) be taken into account when considering the learning task?

8   What would 'reasonable expectations' have been for Savas at various times?

tinct and separate organism. This refers to a capacity for self-consciousness. This we are not born with. At first we have no consciousness of ourselves. We gradually realise that we are separate and separated individuals.

(b)   Lawrence (1981) suggests that there is still lack of consensus regarding a definition of self-concept:

> For William James, the Self was comprised of four parts – the physical self, the material self, the social self, and the spiritual self – and was of a wholly conscious origin. This view is to be contrasted with the psychoanalytical definition which included unconscious processes. Since Freud a vast number of psychologists have attempted to define the concept, notable among these being Allport (1937), Mead (1934), Symonds (1951), Maslow (1968), Cooley (1902), Jourard (1957) and Rogers (1951). Although these writers developed the theme in different ways they were all in agreement with William James' original definition of the self-concept as a

hypothetical construct which is reflexive, i.e., the 'knower' and the 'known' are the same person.

In 1987 Lawrence attempted to clarify the confusion surrounding the term.

> Firstly, the term self-concept is best defined as the sum total of an individual's mental and physical characteristics and his/her evaluation of them . . . it is useful to consider this self-concept as developing in three areas – self image, ideal self and self-esteem. To understand the concept of self-esteem, however it is necessary to define self-image and ideal self . . . Self-concept is the umbrella term under which the other three develop.
>
> (p.1)

(c) In relation to scholastic achievement Gurney (1988) sees self-concept as rapidly becoming recognised as the fourth 'basic', alongside the 3 Rs.

(d) The capacity for self-consciousness in relation to the formation of the self-concept raises the issue of the extent to which a human being is to be defined only in terms of influences of which he is aware. Awareness of self is the distinctive characteristic of man. Katz (1960) suggested that each individual, through contact with significant others, develops an inner core or self-concept.

(e) The self-concept is formed by a process of socialisation by interaction with others and as a result of the feedback of that interaction. 'You are a good boy', 'You are clever', 'You are not as good as your sister'. We learn of ourselves by comparison, by competition and by selection processes.

   The self-concept is related to social skill and like social skill is learned. Failure of social competence leads to rejection, social isolation and subsequently to the formation of a poor self-concept.

(f) Expectancy and the self-fulfilling prophecy play a part in creating the self-concept. There are many sources of expectancy – all different. According to those expectations, we may be one thing to one person and another thing to someone else.

   In relation to expectancy, external and conscious, there may be other reasons why we appear differently in different contexts. Some of these may be related to subjective and internal forces. Perhaps we may need to play a part in certain circumstances in order to create an impression or to mislead people. Perhaps we are not one person but many?

> I contradict myself. I am large. I contain multitudes.
>
> Walt Whitman

(g) Charlton and David (1989) noted the relationships between the self-concept and the pupils' expectations of their future performance:

Expectations reflect the ways in which pupils predict their own performance level. This in turn depends on previous experience. Self-expectation is therefore learned. It is influenced by parents, teachers, and others, who signal their expectations through their interaction with individuals.

(p.73)

(h) The self is multi-faceted. Somerset Maugham asked which is the real me?

There are times when I look over the various parts of my character with perplexity. I recognize that I am made up of several persons and that the person that at the moment has the upper hand will inevitably give place to another. But which is the real one? All of them or none?

(i) The concept of 'The Ideal Self' is built up through identification with significant others throughout life. This is the individual's picture of himself as he would like to be. It is built up through identification with significant others throughout life; it is susceptible to changes and is never beyond reformation. Initially formed it serves as an anchor for behaviour of a certain pattern. It is based on evaluative judgements of others through either direct or indirect experience, past or present. The pupils' relationship with the teacher and with peers 'feeds' his/her self-concept either positively or negatively, which respectively, can enhance or hinder academic achievement.

(j) Operating all the time in relation to our perceptions of others is the process of interpretation. Kelly's Personal Construct Theory points to the fact that while an individual may put a particular interpretation upon a piece of behaviour, another's interpretation is equally valid. Communication is the all important issue in interacting with others successfully and developing self-esteem. Rogers (1951) outlines the skills of communication which can be learned. Such skills are the same as those associated with counselling and the development of the self-concept. Also, the theory of neuro-linguistic functioning has highlighted the importance of positive 'self talk' in relation to enhancing an individual's self-concept. Nevertheless, failure is almost inevitable in life, but it is not failure which produces low self-esteem so much as the way individuals interpret, or significant others react to, the failure. Charlton and David (1989) note:

It is important, however, to note that school achievement is influenced by cognitive ability and the pupil's perception of those abilities.

(p. 73)

(k)   Witter (1988) stresses the need to enhance self-esteem in order to aid academic achievement:

> Recent research has produced much evidence to indicate the need to help children who have developed a low regard of their own work and ability, to establish a positive self image, and to enhance their self esteem, since self concept and especially academic self concept have been shown to be related to academic achievement.
>
> (p. 94)

Witter's research suggests that, according to both pupils and teachers, there are four main strategies for improving self-esteem and enhancing self-concept. First, the learning of new skills. Second, receiving praise for good classwork. Third, to be given tasks which demonstrate trust – in this context 'trust' is seen as 'high regard and reliance upon one personality by another'. Fourth, the ability of the teacher to take time to listen to children's problems.

(l)   Coopersmith (1967) noted the relationship between 'clearly identified rights and privileges', as well as 'defined limits of behaviour' and children with high self-esteem. Children exhibiting low self-esteem need the organisation of a structured and controlled classroom. These observations were supported by Witter's (1988) research which shows that lack of structure and control were strategies that were least likely to increase self-esteem.

(m)   Burns (1982) suggests that teachers can enhance self-concept by:
●   Making the pupil feel supported
●   Making the pupil feel a responsible being
●   Helping each pupil to feel competent
●   Teaching the pupils to set realistic goals
●   Helping the pupils to evaluate themselves realistically
●   Encouraging realistic self-praise.

(n)   Canfield and Wells (1976) detailed 100 ways to improve pupil's self-concepts, while Thayer (1976) outlined strategies to improve experiential learning and affective development.

(o)   Lawrence, in 1987, published 'Enhancing Self Esteem in the Classroom', which aims to help teachers appreciate how they can influence the self-esteem of pupils in the classroom, with practical suggestions on implementation strategies.

(p)   Charlton (1986) showed the positive effects of counselling and operant condition interventions upon locus of control belief. The locus of control concept refers to the extent to which individuals feel they have control over the events and situations which they encounter. Thus pupils exhibiting internal locus of control believe that they have responsibility for their own success or failure while pupils exhibiting external locus of control believe they have no control over such outcomes, but attribute success or failure to external factors such as fate, luck, or chance. He suggested that:

> . . . these findings have important implications for children who, in addition to experiencing learning difficulties, hold external locus of control beliefs. The consequences of classroom strategies intended to promote feelings of internality may encourage children to practise overt classroom strivings likely to facilitate improved academic performance.
>
> (p. 138)

(q) Success in terms of creating a positive self-concept can be seen to be partly dependant upon internal perceptions as well as external factors plus the individual's ability to accommodate both these areas. As Samuel Butler noted in 'The Way of All Flesh':

> All our lives long, every day and every hour, we are engaged in the process of accommodating our changed and unchanged selves to changed and unchanged surroundings; living, in fact, is nothing else than this process of accommodation; when we fail in it a little we are stupid, when we fail flagrantly we are mad, when we suspend it temporarily we sleep, when we give up the attempt altogether we die. In quiet, uneventful lives there is great strain in the process of fusion and accommodation; in other lives there is great strain, but there is also great fusing and accommodating power; in others great strain with little accommodating power. A life will be successful or not according as the power of accommodation is equal to or unequal to the strain of fusing and adjusting internal and external changes.

Much school time is given to working on literacy and oracy skills. However, whether or not time is allocated to work on children's affective functioning too often depends on adventitious encounters with teachers who have been converted to the need to address such areas. It is time – as a profession – that we all recognized, for example, the need to give adequate time to 'working on the self'.

It is iniquitous for us not to undertake this task. As educators, are we called upon to educate the 'whole' child? If not, who looks after the neglected parts?   (Charlton, Jones and Brown, 1990)

2 The learner-centred school

This outlines one school's attempt to meet the increasing number of problems which detract from the quality of provision that we are able to offer. Having spent some time following traditional ways of containing or modifying unacceptable behaviour and attitudes, we finally realised that the answer could only lie in an altogether more radical approach. Rather than continue to devise new ways of coping with what was going wrong and looking for more and better sanctions to apply – a strategy which has proved to be spectacularly ineffective – we should be looking for ways of preventing the problems from arising in the first place.

The school undertook a total review of the curriculum and of all its working practices. Several decisions were reached fairly quickly:

The curriculum should be relevant.
The curriculum must be accessible to all.
The curriculum should be 'success-based'.
Assessment should be both positive and formative.

This gradually led into a philosophy from which the school's current rationale and working practices derive. In simple terms, the philosophy requires that the relationship between teacher and pupil shall be a partnership based on trust, and that the pupil be included in the professional relationship normally reserved for the teacher-to-teacher relationship. It also demands that the curriculum be seen as relevant, be accessible to pupils and that it be delivered in a way that gives the pupils a degree of control, a feeling of ownership and therefore a sense of investment in the work they do.

Pupils' progress through the curriculum is monitored by way of a Record of Achievement. The record contains evidence of the pupils' work and progress in all subject areas in the form of profile statements. These profiles, couched in terms of differentiated statements of achievement, set targets for further development and are negotiated and signed by both pupil and teacher. There is also provision for evidence of extracurricular achievement. Ownership of the Record of Achievement rests with the pupil, and access to it can only be with the pupil's consent. We have managed to devise a system which allows us to honour our contract with the pupils and still be accountable as a school to those who have a legitimate interest in the welfare and progress of our clients.

This has forced us to take a fresh look at how the school is organised and to question the relevance of the hierarchical system of management. The role of the form tutor is crucial to the delivery of the philosophy: the tutor teams – organised on a Year basis – have the task of maintaining the integrity of the philosophy and of protecting the interests of the individual pupils in their care.

The role of the year head, now renamed year co-ordinator, has changed significantly. S/he assumes a player–manager role, acting as form tutor and manager of the year team. This dual role enables the co-ordinator to operate from a position of credibility and therefore of greater strength.

A key management innovation is the formation of the Steering Group, a body which monitors internally the implementation of the philosophy, is made up of representatives of all levels of responsibility, and exercises a considerable degree of delegated authority. All units of work must be validated by the group before being presented for use in the classroom. This validation ensures that the principles of the scheme are adhered to, that the work is both accessible and appropriate to all levels of ability, and that assessment techniques are valid. The Steering Group also appoints form tutors and ensures that appropriate INSET opportunities are made available to staff.

This scheme challenges many of the long-held values, attitudes and expectations to be found both inside and outside schools. To list some of them should provide considerable scope for discussion.

- the pupil is the focus of our endeavours
- the pupil is a person with rights and sensitivities
- staff must accept the need to show vulnerability
- staff can no longer automatically 'close ranks' in times of confrontation
- traditionally perceived status must be redefined in the best interests of the clients and of the philosophy
- curriculum decisions must be subject to a wider consensus than that of the individual department
- standards set must be realistic: unnecessary areas of confrontation must be removed: the relevance of the school's 'rules and regulations' must be challenged
- the organisation, structures and systems within the school must serve the needs of the learning process.

Success has been promoted by

- empowering both pupils and staff, giving both a sense of ownership and an investment in the scheme
- creating small tutor groups
- creating time within existing resources
- maintaining a high profile
- providing high quality INSET
- inbuilt evaluation
- placing process before a product.

It is difficult to condense such a major initiative into such a short space. The experience of this school shows that with the right approach and with the right management structures, the face of education can be changed, even when that change is taking place through a period of great unrest and low morale within the teaching force.

There has been positive feedback from HMI, pupils, staff, year heads, parents and the Monitoring Group.

The Monitoring Group – Composition:
Headteacher   Governor

ICA Co-ordinator   Secondary Headteacher
Year Head   Primary Headteacher
Special Needs   Adviser
Pupil   Representative from FE
Parent   Secretary of the Local Employers' Network

 The existence of the Monitoring Group is an indication of the school's confidence in its undertaking. The group meets formally once per term, and in addition individual members of the group visit the school to evaluate the scheme. This is achieved by discussion with staff and pupils and by visiting lessons. All evaluation documents are negotiated with the relevant people, and so far no one in the school has felt the need to restrict the audience. The group has a dual role, providing an external perception of the scheme, as well as acting as a vehicle for disseminating our work out into the community.

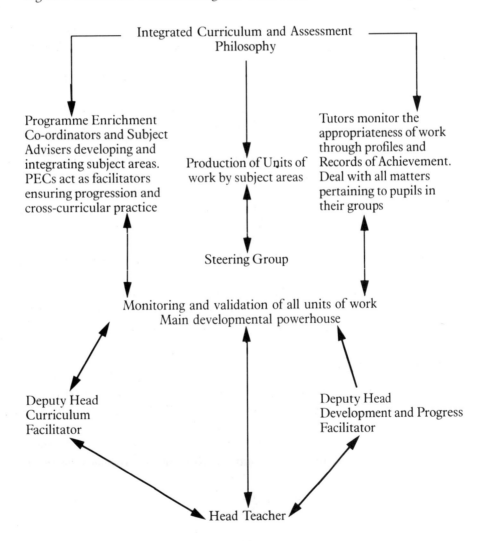

3 'Killer' statements by teachers

Recalled from their schooldays by teachers attending an In-Service Training day on self-concepts.

. . . belittled me for doing badly in the class History test. I took the test after a weekend when our house had been burgled, and my mother was taken suddenly into hospital. When I explained all this, I was given an aspirin and told to stop crying.

. . . who had taught me French for the previous four years, asked me what my name was, and if I was new to the school.

. . . commented on my 'unusually' good French homework and said, 'I suppose your father did this'. I decided it wasn't worth trying anymore.

. . . kept me in class after a German lesson, and punched me in the stomach with the text book for doing badly in a German test.

. . . said, 'You won't get your 'O' levels, never mind get to university'.

. . . laughed about me (in front of me), with the Headmaster, when my mother had just been to the school.

. . . remarked that my low test score was just what he expected from a 'council house' child.

. . . decided that I was too untidy to stand on the stage and sing in the choir at the Christmas Carol Service.

. . . said, 'You're nearly as stupid as your brother; if that's possible!'

. . . told me to stand on the stage and show the school the long stockings I was wearing (they were not allowed). He said that I looked like a wrinkled, old woman. He then got the whole school to clap at his 'joke'.

4 Useful reading

ALLPORT, B. (1937) *Personality: A Psychological Interpretation* (New York: Holt).

BARON, A.R. and BYRNE, D. (1977) *Social Psychology: Understanding Human Interaction* (London: Allyn and Bacon).

BURNS, R.B. (1977) 'The Self Concept and Its Relevance to Academic Achievement', in Child, D. *Readings in Psychology for the Teacher* (London: Holt, Rinehart and Winston).

BURNS, R.B. (1982) *Self Concept Development and Education* (New York: Holt, Rinehart and Winston).

CANFIELD, J. and WELLS, H.C. (1976) *100 Ways to Enhance the Self Concept in the classroom: A handbook for Teachers and Parents* (New Jersey: Prentice Hall).

CHARLTON, T. (1985) 'Locus of Control as a therapeutic strategy for helping children with behaviour and learning problems', *Maladjustment and Therapeutic Education*, 3 (1), 26–32.

CHARLTON, T. (1986) 'Differential Effects of counselling and Operant Conditioning Interventions upon Children's Locus of Reinforcement Control Beliefs' in *Psychological Reports*, 59, pp. 137–8.

CHARLTON, T. and DAVID, K. (1989) *Managing Misbehaviour* (Basingstoke: Macmillan Education).

CHARLTON, T., JONES, K. and BROWN, B. (1990) *Working on the 'Self'* (Cheltenham: College of St Paul and St Mary).

COOLEY, C.H. (1902) *Human Nature and the Social Order* (New York: Scribener).

COOPERSMITH, S. (1967) *The Antecedents of Self Esteem* (San Francisco and London: Freeman and Co.).

GURNEY, P. (1988) *Self Esteem in Children with Special Educational Needs* (London: Routledge).

JOURARD, S. (1957) 'Identification, parent-cathesis and self-esteem', *Journal of Consultant Psychology*, 21, pp. 375–80.

KATZ, D. (1960) 'The Functional Approach to the Study of Attitude Change', *Public Opinion Quarterly*, No. 24, pp. 163–204.

LAWRENCE, D. (1973) *Improved Reading Through Counselling* (London: Ward Lock).

LAWRENCE, D. (1981) 'The Development of a Self-Esteem Questionnaire' in *The British Journal of Educational Psychology*, 51, p. 245–51.

LAWRENCE, D. (1987) *Enhancing Self-Esteem in the Classroom* (London: PCP Education Series).

MASLOW, A. (1968) *Towards a Psychology of Being* (New York: Van Nostrand Reinhold).

MEAD, G.H. (1934) *Mind, Self and Society* (Chicago, University of Chicago Press).

MCDAVID, J.W. and HARARI, H. (1968) *Psychology and Social Behaviour* (London: Harper and Row).

MILLER, R. (1985) Unpublished notes from a lecture given on the Self Concept (The College of St Paul and St Mary, Cheltenham).

NIAS, J. (1987) 'Teaching the Self' in *Cambridge Journal of Education*, Vol. 17, No. 3, p. 178–85.

ROGERS, C. (1951) *Client Centred Therapy* (Boston: Houghton-Mifflin).

SYMONDS, P.M. (1951) *The Ego and the Self* (New York: Appleton-Century Crofts).

THOMAS, J. (1980) *The Self in Education* (Windsor: NFER).

WITTER, G. (1988) 'To See Ourselves as Others See Us'. *Support for Learning*, Vol. 3, No. 2, May, p. 93–8.

CASE STUDY 15

Clearview High School

*In-Service Training in Personal
and Social Education*

This case study is based on an imaginary school, but is typical of many training sessions held in a variety of state and private secondary schools. All the details have occurred in actual training days, and this amalgam provides material for discussion by school teachers and students in basic training.

Clearview is a Comprehensive High School of approaching 700 pupils, and with a sixth form. It serves a large council housing estate, as well as an area of private suburban housing and a fringe rural area with smallholdings and a scattering of light industrial development.

The school was a secondary modern school in the 1960s but now has had a long comprehensive history, and is regarded with respect and even mild affection by local people. Its academic record is modest, and discipline has been good until the last year or two, when many new staff have been appointed as older senior staff have retired.

The Headteacher was appointed less than two years ago, after a career spanning both grammar and comprehensive school experience. He is a quiet determined man with strong views of collegiate leadership – he likes to work by delegation and influence, rather than by a charismatic approach. There are three Deputy Headteachers with responsibilities for (a) administration and the sixth-form centre, (b) curriculum and senior pupils, and (c) pastoral care and development, and junior pupils.

A series of staff working parties has functioned for just under a year, comprising a mixture of senior and junior staff, with a brief to study and recommend development in (A) pupils' personal and social development (B) curriculum development, and (C) staff development. The working parties A and C had requested a training day for the staff, based on three factors:

(a) personal development of pupils and records
(b) tutorial work and pastoral care programmes
(c) staff pastoral care training.

A training day had been agreed by the local authority, and, exceptionally, permission had been given for expenditure on a residential setting at a conference hotel. This would be followed by a further day's training in school, and later voluntary sessions for staff in evenings.

Working party B had agreed that part of their remit lay in the proposed residential session, and agreed their further requirements would be met in the following training periods. Most of the staff were pleased and intrigued with the planning, though a smaller group of younger teachers appeared less co-operative. One of the Deputy Headteachers, the most senior in age and service, was agreeable but cynical.

The Headteacher, working with his local authority advisory officer and also with his helpful and enthusiastic chairman of managers, a factory manager, had to decide whether to manage the training days himself, or to use local advisory staff, HMI, colleagues from other schools, staff from a College of Higher Education or the more distant university, or other consultant contributors. He decided on using an outside consultant for the first session.

The consultant was recommended to the Headteacher, and was approached first by telephone. After further correspondence and telephone conversations a draft plan was submitted and commented on by senior staff, and by the working party chairmen who were middle-grade teachers.

A final programme was eventually agreed and this and hand-out material was photocopied, given an attractive cover, and prepared for issue to all staff.

The residential conference was timetabled as follows.

Thursday   Meet at the hotel at 5.30 p.m.
Session I – 6.30–7.15 p.m.
In this session the three working party chairmen discussed the work of their groups, the visits they had made to other schools, and the books and research they had considered. The Headteacher then summed up his impressions and expectations.

Arranged inter-disciplinary discussion groups followed after dinner, concentrating largely on the curriculum working party comments, and their implications for the staff.

Friday   Session II – 9.15–10.30 a.m.
A presentation by the consultant on pupils' physical, intellectual and emotional development, on school–family relationships, on counselling and referral and support agencies.

Session III – 11.00 a.m.–12.15 p.m.
A presentation on tutorial work and academic guidance.

Session IV – 2.0–3.15 p.m.
A presentation on pastoral care administration, on school records, on staff pastoral and academic team planning, and on the individual responses of staff to these professional matters.

Each presentation was kept brief, was supported by hand-out material for later discussion and development, and was broken by a variety of informal short discussions on various points.

Session V – 3.15–5.00 p.m.
Arranged discussion groups based on pastoral teams, and concluding with a general forum, with the consultant and senior staff responding to questions and viewpoints.

Follow-up work in subsequent weeks consisted of an evaluation study of the conference, and further working party discussions, meetings with parents and managers, and the publishing of a 'Pastoral report'. This included statements of the school's planning in personal and social education, including health and sex education, in discipline and in guidance matters.

At the second In-Service Training day held at the school the programme was as follows.

Session I. Reflections on the pastoral report by a local authority adviser, and a 'situation report' by the Deputy Headteachers.

Session II. Academic achievement – a presentation by a College of Higher Education lecturer.

Session III. Discussions on Session II, and a summing up by the Headteacher.

Session IV. Discussions led by members of the curriculum working party.

The final part of this In-Service Training package comprised the following:

(a) A further evaluation report on the second day's training.

(b) A further series of meetings by academic departments on profiling, and with concentration on the link between teaching methods and academic achievement.

(c) A voluntary six-session evening course on counselling, led by a Relate tutor.

(d) A seminar for seven senior staff on school management, led by the Headteacher and a colleague Headteacher from another school.

(e) A voluntary six-session evening course on 'Active Tutorial Work' organised by the local authority.

QUESTIONS

1   What improvements in this package could you recommend, and why? How much is also appropriate in Primary School In-Service Training?

2   What major differences would affect the way your school planned such an In-Service series?

3   Should selected pupils or interested parents and managers usefully be invited to attend such sessions?

4   Are such sessions too demanding on teachers?

5   What exactly does 'staff development' imply?

6   Which of the following training concepts or skills could be included in a school's In-Service plans?

- Working parties of staff dealing with a topic.
- Individual teachers reporting to staff meetings on books, courses, educational news items.
- Staff appraisal schemes.
- Certain Open University modules.
- Sociometry and study skills.
- Links with, and parallel training of, ancillary staff.
- The use of visitors to lead staff discussions, or to be 'interviewed' and looked after by groups of pupils.
- Links with Further Education and Primary Schools.
- Social and Life Skills material.
- Active Tutorial Work material.

7   How much of this material is suitable for use in pre-service training?

SUPPORTIVE INFORMATION AND MATERIAL

IN-SERVICE HANDOUT A P

1   The tutor

The form tutors are the foundation of the pastoral team and the success of such teams can usually be measured by the quality of the school's tutorial work, and the pupils' respect for it. It is essential that tutors should build up a close knowledge of their pupils, sharing this information as appropriate with the senior colleagues who have overall responsibility for the academic and social development of each pupil.

2   Aims and objectives

An individual exercise. Mark your order of priority of the following aims of tutorial work. Later, share your feelings with a colleague whom you do not often meet.

Care	Building community feeling		Monitoring individual development	Discipline
	Order	Information about pupils		Good relationships with teacher
Encouraging learning				
	Feeling of security		Observing pupils	
Co-ordinated programme of discussion work		Personal and social education		Encouraging judgement and decision-making
Monitoring homework	Welfare		Avoiding trouble	

3   Tutorial concepts and requirements

(i)   Good tutorial work is part of the nature of teaching.

(ii)   It is about relationships, talking with pupils, listening and not always interrogating.

(iii) The tutor is a negotiator on behalf of his or her group, a link and liaison with other staff.

(iv)   The group provides some security and family feeling – trust and loyalty can be developed.

(v)   School administrative matters, and information and records can be kept by the tutor.

(vi)   The tutor's regular observation of pupils' development is important.

(vii) Discipline can be dealt with at tutorial level.

(viii) It provides a link with parents perhaps.

(ix)   The group can be the first line in observation of the whole range of a pupil's achievements, as distinct from departmental observation of a particular subject. There can be periodic 'interviews' with individual pupils or groups of pupils, in which all-round standards of work are discussed.

(x) In tutorial periods there can usually be found time to have anything from 10 to 30 minutes of discussion on prepared topics of personal and social education, or on school matters or problems.

4 Tutorial organisation

(a) A school *co-ordinator* of tutorial work, and of tutorial discussion programmes, will be appointed.

(b) *Team approach* – a repertoire of skills is needed among the team of teachers dealing with a particular year group – counselling, discussion and groupwork, careers guidance, study, administration, health education, personal and social education, and active tutorial work skills and experience. Tutors can take each other's groups at times.

(c) Programmes of discussion work need *preparation*, and prepared *materials.*

(d) *Differing personalities* among staff contribute in different ways.

(e) There may be *priorities* laid down by the local authority, Governors, Headteacher.

(f) *Records* are sometimes kept by tutors, or are contributed to by tutors.

(g) Teachers have *dual roles – academic and pastoral*, and these must be discussed and understood.

(h) The *size of tutorial groups* requires planning and school policy. How many staff are exempted from tutorial duties, and why?

(i) The *time* arranged for tutorial work is a matter of school policy, and depends on the quality of pastoral planning and preparation.

(j) Pupils' *problems* require a team approach, with differing levels of counselling, and with referral and support systems planned and operating efficiently to support staff.

(k) The skills of *counselling and of interviewing* may be seen as different.

IN-SERVICE HANDOUT B P|

Discussion material for tutorial periods

(a) *School organisation* and the main points of its philosophy.

(b) *Roles* of Headmaster, Deputy Headmaster, senior master/mistress, heads of departments, year tutors, class tutors, office staff, ancillary staff.

(c) Discussion on *communities*; the school and the local community.

(d) The need for *school rules*; detailed explanations and reasons. Good *manners*; reasons and how measured.

(e) Explanation of *school information* procedures; communication as a key to the smooth running of the school; the importance of communication with parents; link with communication in the community – how people are informed.

(f) Information about *extracurricular activities*; local leisure opportunities.

(g) Election of pupil representatives to House/Year/School *councils*; agendas; positive and negative contributions discussed; value and difficulties of consultation. What are the limits? What can we be democratic about?

(h) Support for *school functions*.

(i) Discussion of *occasional group activities* such as a visit to the theatre or a concert; making class wall magazines; tape-recorded magazines for exchange with other classes or schools; class scrapbooks.

(j) Themes for class/school *assemblies* prepared.

(k) *Educational choices* in school; personal options debated; standards discussed.

(l) The use of *libraries* – study skills and habits.

(m) Opportunities and need for service; support for charities; community service.

(n) *Careers* information and discussions.

(o) *Interviewing* invited people – school staff and outsiders. Questions are prepared beforehand and discussion follows the visit.

(p) Personal *appearance*, cleanliness, dress.

(q) Reading and listening to *human relationships themes* referred to in appropriate poems and stories; teacher contributing, pupils contributing.

(r) *Films* in local cinema discussed.

(s) *Television* programmes discussed.

(t) Magazines and newspaper cuttings for discussion.

(u) News items.

(v) *Local problems* – vandalism, etc.

(w) *Family* holiday/leisure/moving plans.

(x) How do we identify with class, with the school, with community? What does 'belonging' mean?

Personal awareness of each child
- of himself/herself
- of himself/herself within family
- of himself/herself within the form group, and with his peers
- of himself/herself in the larger year group
- of himself/herself in the local community.

(y) Friendships in the class, group and school, the need to give as well as take, and loneliness and the needs of others.

(z) Personal interviews with pupils.

IN-SERVICE HANDOUT C 🅿

1 Tutorial activities

Observation of others	Questioning about an attitude
Individuals or groups to provide 'a solution' to a problem	Class discussions – and smaller group discussions
Community involvement	Interviewing visitors
Dramatisation and artwork	Cartoons on social matters
Simulation exercises	Visits
Role-play	Buzz groups – 'off the cuff' though
Media imitation	Brains trust
Audio visual aids material – tape school newspaper	Committee work
Written work – worksheets – leaflets	Individual and group presentations on a theme
Questionnaires	Displays
Projects, research and surveys	Reflection and quiet
Debates	Case studies explored

2 Possible visitors to tutorial groups, and referral agencies

See material under Case Study 12 'Wendy'.

IN-SERVICE HANDOUT D 🅿 (1–3)

1 Long-term objectives in tutorial work

(a) Work skills

To develop the ability to plan and use time effectively.
To develop the ability to plan a simple method of enquiry, or piece of action research.

To develop skill in communicating ideas orally and in writing.
To develop the ability to work independently and co-operatively, as required.

(b) Personal Skills

To develop the acceptance of a 'realistic' self-picture.
To develop skill in conversation in a variety of situations, including the ability to listen.
To develop the ability to make contacts; to take initiatives in meeting people and to develop flexibilities of response.

(c) Group Skills

To develop skill in listening and gauging the feelings of others in the group.
To develop skill in assessing the reactions of others to one's own behaviour.
To develop the ability to defer judgment and allow for a variety of viewpoints and feelings.

2   Pupils' personal development topics

Differing rates of puberty.
Growth spurts among boys and girls.
Body image and sensitivity of pupils to size and appearance.
Adolescent anxiety.
Sexual maturation, physical and emotional.
Personality development.
Temperament.
Diet and overweight pupils, anorexia, malnutrition.
Signs of illness, neglect or injury, tiredness, lack of sleep.
Eyesight and hearing difficulties.
Health problems: eczema, asthma, epilepsy, dyslexia, acne and skin cleanliness.
Clumsiness and effect of birth difficulties.
Changes in mood.
Family effect: only child, large families, only boy or girl in family, youngest or oldest in family, racial and class attitudes.
Effect of peer group and friendships.
Attendance and appearance as signs of attitude.

3   Normal tasks of adolescence

Puberty
Independence
Emotions
Sexuality
Intelligence
Physical growth and maturity
Self-consciousness and temporary moods and worries

Relationships with family and relatives
Relationships with contemporaries
Social competence and coping skills and attitudes
The values and boundaries of behaviour which have been absorbed
Learning skills and achievement attitudes.

4   Life skills lists

Lifeskills Teaching Programmes, Lifeskills Associates Ltd, Leeds. (See p. 128).

5   Useful reading

BALDWIN, J. and WELLS, H. (1979–83) *Active Tutorial Work* (Oxford: Blackwell).
BLACKBURN, K. (1975) *The Tutor* (London: Heinemann).
BUTTON, L. (1982) *Group Tutoring for the Form Tutor* (London: Hodder and Stoughton).
CHARLTON, T. and DAVID, K. (1989) *Managing Misbehaviour* (Basingstoke: Macmillan Education).
DAVID, K. (1982) *Personal & Social Education in Secondary Schools* (London: Longman).
HAMBLIN, D. (1986) *A Pastoral Programme* (Oxford: Blackwell).
HOPSON, B. and SALLY, M. (1979) *Life Skills Teaching Programme* (Leeds: Life Skills Associates).
SCHOOLS COUNCILS (SCHEP) (1982) *Health Education 13–18. Introductory Handbook* (London: Forbes).
TEACHERS' ADVISORY COUNCIL ON ALCOHOL AND DRUG EDUCATION (1986) *Skills for Adolescence* (Salford: TACADE).
MCGUINESS, J. (1982) *Planned Pastoral Care* (London: McGraw Hill).

LIFESKILLS: TAKING CHARGE OF YOURSELF AND YOUR LIFE

ME

Skills I Need to Manage and Grow

- how to read and write
- how to achieve basic numeracy
- how to find information and resources
- how to think and solve problems constructively
- how to identify my creative potential and develop it
- how to manage time effectively
- how to make the most of the present
- how to discover my interests
- how to discover my values and beliefs
- how to set and achieve goals
- how to take stock of my life
- how to discover what makes me do the things I do
- how to be positive about myself
- how to cope with and gain from life transitions
- how to make effective decisions
- how to be proactive
- how to manage negative emotions
- how to cope with stress
- how to achieve and maintain physical well-being
- how to manage my sexuality

ME AND YOU

Skills I Need to Relate Effectively to You

- how to communicate effectively
- how to make, keep and end a relationship
- how to give and get help
- how to manage conflict
- how to give and receive feedback

ME AND OTHERS

Skills I Need to Relate Effectively to Others

- how to be assertive
- how to influence people and systems
- how to work in groups
- how to express feelings constructively
- how to build strengths in others

ME AND SPECIFIC SITUATIONS

Skills I Need For My Education

- how to discover the education options open to me
- how to choose a course
- how to study

Skills I Need At Work

- how to discover the job options open to me
- how to find a job
- how to keep a job
- how to change jobs
- how to cope with unemployment
- how to achieve a balance between my job and the rest of my life
- how to retire and enjoy it

Skills I Need At Home

- how to choose a style of living
- how to maintain a home
- how to live with other people

Skills I Need At Leisure

- how to choose between leisure options
- how to maximise my leisure opportunities
- how to use my leisure to increase my income

Skills I Need in the Community

- how to be a skilled consumer
- how to develop and use my political awareness
- how to use public facilities

© Lifeskills Associates Ltd, Leeds. From Lifeskills Teaching Programmes.